The College Student

THE LIBRARY OF EDUCATION

A Project of The Center for Applied Research in Education, Inc.

G. R. Gottschalk, Director

Categories of Coverage

I	II	III
Curriculum and Teaching	Administration, Organization, and Finance	Psychology for Educators

IV	V	VI
History, Philosophy, and Social Foundations	Professional Skills	Educational Institutions

The College Student

WILBUR B. BROOKOVER

DAVID GOTTLIEB
IRVIN J. LEHMANN
ROBERT RICHARDS
J. FRED THADEN
ARTHUR M. VENER

The Center for Applied Research in Education, Inc.
New York

LIBRARY OF CONGRESS
CATALOG CARD NO.: 65-20310

Foreword

The present volume is a contribution to the growing research literature on American college and university students. The interest this work represents is of long standing, although the forms the discussion has taken have paralleled changes in the character of the social sciences. From the anecdotal, speculative, and philosophical reflections on the nature of students, which are as old as—and indeed a part of—higher education itself, the development has been steadily toward a more systematic and empirical study of college students and the institutions they attend.

Students comprise an ideal body of subjects for most kinds of social research. They are a literate, compliant, and captive population for survey research; they are inexpensive and available subjects for experiments; they have been gathered together in readily accessible places for systematic observation; some of their characteristics have been recorded systematically over time by institutions, by states, and by the federal government and are available to demographers and social statisticians. And thousands of social scientists have exploited the existing data about students as well as the ease of access to students in their own institutions.

Much of this work has not added to knowledge about college and university students because it has ignored the fact that the students *were* students and has dealt with them as a convenient set of human beings. Sherif's famous experiment on social influences on perception was carried out with student subjects, yet tells us nothing about students qua students. By contrast, other investigators whose primary interests were in theoretical and even methodological problems have advanced knowledge of student life and characteristics. For example, the studies of Hanan Selvin and his collaborators on student residence halls, motivated primarily by a broader interest in the influences of social contexts on individual and group behaviors, nevertheless reveals a good deal about student life and culture.[1] We are now beginning to see more research focused on organizational structure and process. In this work, the institution reveals its internal processes through the way in which it deals with the various kinds of students it admits, retains, or extrudes at various points in their college careers; the students function in the research as a kind of barium tracer, throwing into bold relief otherwise obscure aspects of the institution. Here, too, increased knowledge about students is a by-product of an interest in other matters—in this case, organizational theory.

---

[1] See Hanan C. Selvin and Warren O. Hagstrom, "Determinants at Support for Civil Liberties," *British Journal of Sociology*, 11:1 (March 1960), 51–73.

A very different source of interest in college students is the rapid growth of higher education and the many practical administrative and pedagogical problems to which large numbers give rise. The growth and democratization of higher education brings to our colleges large numbers of students whose values and purposes are unfamiliar to academic men. Moreover, conditions in the large public colleges and universities especially make it difficult to establish the old personal relation of student and teacher. It becomes increasingly difficult, as both student numbers and research opportunities grow, for the faculty member to know his anonymous students in any real sense. And, increasingly, educators turn to social science to tell them the facts about their students that they can no longer gain through their own experience in classroom or administrative office.

The growth in student numbers, coupled with the rapidity of change in the academic world, generates a demand for expert and systematic knowledge that social research seems able to supply. But over and above that is the stimulus to research that flows from another aspect of the democratization of higher education—that is, the new forms that "public accountability" take for the many institutions, both public and private, now heavily dependent on public funds and support. The democratization of education is not merely a matter of growing numbers or the increasing application of universalistic criteria of achievement by admissions offices; it is also reflected in the growing obligation of colleges and universities to justify their practices by reference to the public good. To do that convincingly, even private institutions can rely less and less on unconfirmed assessments of their educational programs. It is not enough these days that colleges and universities act in the public interest; they must also be *seen* to do so—and how better than through the evidence produced by social science research on their campuses?

There are other powerful, if more directly practical, stimuli to research on college and university students. One of these, the relatively new concern with national educational policy and higher education, reflects both the rapid expansion of the system and the growing recognition of the close connection between higher education and national power. The trends and projections of college enrollments developed in Chapter VI are of interest to many audiences: to economists concerned with the labor force and the occupational structure; to administrators and politicians concerned with future demands for resources for higher education and research; to educators concerned with the recruitment and training of college teachers, to political scientists interested in the bearing of the rapid rise in the educational attainment of the American population on the future direction of public opinion and public policy.

The practical implications of student studies are as great on the institutional as on the societal level. Studies of student subcultures, discussed in Chapter V, are of the greatest relevance and interest of educators who want to strengthen and upgrade their institutions. The nature and relative strength of the several student subcultures on any given campus may be more easily modified by administrators and faculty than is the character of a (largely tenured) faculty or the curriculum it so jealously guards. And many college presidents, deans, admissions officers, and student personnel people are interested in the ways in which their policies might be used to reshape the intellectual and academic climate.

Much research on college students is closely and ambiguously involved with educational policy; the research on student selection discussed in Chapter IV is a case in point. Such research raises many moral and political questions, as well as technical and scientific ones. Indeed, a problem area very much in need of study involves the ways in which research and practice in education react on each other. To what extent is educational practice influenced by research? More specifically, what parts of educational practice are responsive or highly resistant to research findings, and how can we account for the differences? The extent to which research touches on strongly held values or on sensitive points of interest or power in an institution will certainly affect its reception by the institution and its effects on educational practice. And the relation of the researcher to the institution in which he conducts his studies is only one of the important variables affecting what he studies, what he finds out, and what consequences his findings have for the institution. Answers to such questions may have significance for a much broader range of social research and much wider fields of social action.

As the senior author notes in Chapter I, this volume does not aim to be a summary of contemporary knowledge about American college and university students, nor does it attempt to touch on all aspects of higher education which bear on the characteristics and behavior of students. But the volume does show something of the range of interests represented in the study of college students, and helps to point out where some of the most pressing research problems lie.

MARTIN TROW

Department of Sociology
University of California

The College Student
Wilbur B. Brookover

One of the major educational developments during the past fifty years is the system of higher education which has grown up in the United States and which is still expanding at a fantastic rate. Various aspects of the system including information about the college environment, the college student, and college and university administration are presented in separate volumes of the Library of Education. Dr. Brookover and several of his colleagues have collaborated in *The College Student* to give a detailed picture of the clientele which the system serves, specifying changes in their numbers, characteristics, and objectives over the past century.

Dr. Brookover, Director of the Social Science Teaching Institute and Professor of Sociology and Education, Michigan State University, is particularly well qualified to head the team of educators and sociologists, who contributed the various chapters. An eclectic approach has been used which permits an examination of contemporary American college students with sufficient historical background to recognize changing patterns of college life. Psychological and sociological research, some of which is still going on, is used effectively.

ERIC GARDNER
Content Editor

Contents

ix

CONTENTS

CHAPTER I

Introduction

WILBUR B. BROOKOVER

Director, Social Science
Teaching Institute
Professor, Sociology and
Education

This monograph has been designed to examine contemporary American college students, providing sufficient historical perspective to reveal the changing patterns of college life. The rapidly expanding student population is associated with changes in the social and educational background of students, the function of higher education in the society, the pattern of college organization, the impact of college on the student, and the integration of the college in the occupational structure of the society. The purpose here is to analyze college students as a particular segment of American society, to examine relevant college policies, and to assess the impact of the college on student behavior and on their subsequent positions in society.

The authors have drawn on several behavioral science disciplines as well as education, but sociology and social psychology provide the basic framework for our description and analysis. Our goal, therefore, is to provide a brief analysis of the college student in American society and the function of higher education in the society.

Behavioral scientists in colleges and universities have recently completed several significant analyses of higher education, and centers for the study of higher education have been established. This interest in education probably emerges in part from the contemporary debates and general public discussion of American education. In response to public concern about educational needs, both public and private agencies have provided resources to support research designed to answer many questions about education.

Recently, a wide range of studies of higher education have been produced. Several studies of the impact of college experience on student values provide evidence of differential impact among colleges and subgroups of students within a given student body. These

1

stimulated more refined analysis of college subcultures and the specific impact of various student groups. These studies are reflected in Chapters V and VI of this monograph.

The analysis of college student populations, the projection of future enrollments, and the need for faculty, buildings and other facilities have been the foci of much research in recent years. Except for the basic demographic analysis in Chapter III, this monograph does not reflect this important body of research. The composition of the college student population is an important variable in understanding college students, but the problems of providing faculty and facilities for expanding higher education are not examined here.

Perhaps the most extensive body of research is concerned with the prediction of success in college. The first of these studies occurred several decades ago, but the recent press of college students on available facilities has greatly enhanced the efforts to find adequate predictive criteria of success. Although these research findings have not been reviewed here, they provide a basis for the discussion of admission policies and procedures in Chapter III.

Another important area of research has been concerned with the function of higher education in the choice of, and persistence in, post-college careers. Although the importance of liberal education is emphasized, most Americans perceive college education as preparation for some occupational roles. The growing demand for college-educated personnel in the labor force has highlighted the importance of this function of higher education. Chapter VII reviews some research in this area and analyzes the process by which college students are allocated to various positions in society.

The monograph is the work of several colleagues at Michigan State University. Although they are identified with several different units of the University, all are behavioral scientists interested in the analysis of educational institutions and processes.

The chapter topics and broad outlines were planned by the senior author, but each author developed his chapter as he wished. This practice, of course, resulted in some variation in style and organizational pattern, but provided the optimum arrangement for each scholar to analyze the topic selected.

CHAPTER II

The College Student in Changing America

ROBERT RICHARDS

Instructor, Social Science

Young man home from college makes a big display
With a great big jaw-break that he can hardly say.
It can't be found in Webster's and won't be for a while
But we know he's only puttin' on the style.
Folk tune of the 1880's[1]

What did the college student of the past think of the world around him? Where and how did he fit himself into the world? And what did he want out of that world?

Such questions are unanswered in early college annals; therefore they can be answered only inferentially. The student's behavior is evident; from it, his attitudes must be surmised.

Glimpses of student life in the past reveal changes paralleling momentous transformations in American life. This cultural evolution was not characterized by consistent change; the Industrial Revolution promulgated a plethora of social change in the mid-nineteenth century, culminating in dynamic upheavals in American business and economy after the Civil War.

The post-Civil War period serves as a historical fulcrum for much of that which unfolds later in the life and thought of contemporary American college students.

Some collegiate interests cut across time, social class, and geography. Through these universal interests—campus life and campus groups, manners and morals, men and women, religion and politics, prospects and expectations—student life reflects the dominant social movements in American history.

---

[1] Pete Seeger, *American Favorite Ballads* (New York: Oak Publications, 1961), p. 68.

The College Student in
Preindustrial America[2]

Campus life and campus groups.   An anthropologist dropped on the campus of any early American college would have discovered life there as exotic as that on any South Sea island.

For example, he would have observed "clans" within the "tribe" which oriented student loyalties, values, and status. There were usually four such clans: freshmen, sophomores, juniors, and seniors. These labels remain a part of campus lexicon, but today they have only vestigial social significance among students and are of primary concern only to curriculum planners and varsity coaches.

Within these clans, friendships were formed, honors grasped, and battles fought. Class domination of student life was dramatized during commencement, an annual ritual quite different from the solemn exercises of today. Over a period of several days, seniors demonstrated their readiness to enter the adult arena by expounding at length in Greek. This impressed and entertained lowerclassmen, townspeople, visiting dignitaries, sweethearts, and occasionally passing groups of Indians.

Why did classes become the nucleus of colonial campus life? The significance of the four classes, and many other campus customs and institutions, represents adoption of informal procedures to the formal educational structure. The class system evolved out of the requirements of the classical curriculum, which typically prescribed a set program for each year: Greek and Latin, rhetoric, and mathematics the first two years; natural philosophy (physics, chemistry) in the third year; logic, metaphysics, ethics, and evidences of Christianity in the fourth year. The young scholars found they shared a common cause as they battled Euclid or Cicero. This bond created the clan-like unity of the class which pervaded all student life.

The curriculum which spawned this social system was, in turn, a product of the most popular rationalization for decision-making throughout the history of American colleges: tradition. One is left to ponder the practicality of a classical curriculum inherited from Oxford and Cambridge for the preparation of the leaders and builders of a frontier society.

---

2 Historical material for the following sections, unless otherwise noted, was drawn from the following sources: Ernest Earnest, *Academic Procession* (New York: Bobbs-Merrill Company, Inc., 1953); Henry D. Sheldon, *Student Life and Customs* (New York: Appleton-Century-Crofts, 1901).

The classroom reflected issues of the Roman Republic more accurately than it did those of the new-born American republic. Students eager to argue found no platform in the classroom; comradeship was all the school class system could provide. Thus, classes were superseded by debate societies as the foundation of campus social life. For fifty years after the American Revolution, campuses resounded with fervent argument over every issue from God's authorship of sin to the tax on hogs. The societies frequently generated more heat than light, a condition not unfamiliar in the history of American oratory.

Not as purveyors of dubious forensics did debate societies make their principal contribution to American campus life. They were primarily social clubs, "rushing" likely candidates much as modern fraternities recruit members. Contrasting sharply with the bleak campus dormitories, the quarters of the debate societies sported elaborate lounges, and the private libraries maintained by these societies often outstripped those operated by colleges themselves.

Debate topics were often superficial, and oratorical skill outshown profundity. But because classroom experience was frequently more stultifying than stimulating, debating clubs provided the only opportunity for many students to review issues related to their lives as citizens. And of course the clubs were crucial training grounds for the young elite to adopt the public posture of their adult years.

Athletics were conspicuous by their absence on these early campuses. Frowned upon by faculties, athletics did not attain much popularity among students as a pathway to campus glory. Avid sportsmen were tolerated, but certainly not lionized.

If athletic prowess did not mark the "big man on campus," neither did scholarly diligence. Some studied harder than others, but few found academic demands so onerous as to unduly limit an active social life. An "all-round good fellow" was the ideal—and he was probably so defined by his social adroitness rather than by his familiarity with natural philosophy.

Manners and morals. No aspect of campus life is the object of as much public scrutiny as student morality—or its suspected absence. Student character has been castigated by journalists, by clergymen, and even by academicians. Charles Nisbet, President of Dickinson College in 1793, characterized his students as "indolent . . . , vain . . . , lazy, . . . averse to reading or thinking."[3]

---

[3] "Charles Nisbet Complains of Lazy Students and Educational Quacks," in Richard Hofstadter and Wilson Smith, *American Higher Education* (Chicago: The University of Chicago Press, 1961), Vol. I, p. 254.

The coarse life of the frontier did not stop at the campus gates. Students blew up dormitories, desecrated presidents' homes, and assaulted faculty. Changes in pedagogy or curriculum could set off full-scale rebellions. And if that would not do it, bad food would. Rebel students sometimes "captured" the campus, but invariably the insurrections were quelled, and in some cases a majority of the student body was summarily expelled.

College administrations fought back with a staggering mass of regulations which established theoretical control over every aspect of student life. Students complained that faculties acted as policemen more than pedagogues. As a cure for student impudence, sermons were diligently applied in dosages as large as fourteen services a week.

Young, ebullient students; harsh discipline, rigorously enforced; puritannical religious practices: when wedded to a tedious, irrelevant curriculum, these instruments for inducing control became instruments for inciting chaos.

Despite this turbulence and boisterousness, early campus culture should not be mistaken with that of a frontier lumber camp. Debate societies generated an intellectual atmosphere of sorts, and students did occasional reading on their own. The propriety of novels was questioned, which probably enhanced their popularity. A varied social life was enjoyed; "calling" on girls was a favorite pastime.

Men and women. Higher education for most women was obtainable only in women's academies which were little more, and frequently less, than "finishing schools." Coeducation was not unheard of, for it was a frequent and controversial topic. Almost from their beginnings western schools such as Antioch and Oberlin accepted both sexes. Girls did not suffer from competition with boys; in fact, women sometimes showed up their male peers to be the scholastically weaker sex.

Students at coeducational schools "dated," and by the 1850's Oberlin professors were muttering that their students saw more of each other than of their textbooks. This dating was casual and unself-conscious, with frequent changes in partners.

Sexual relations were regulated by a multiple standard—certainly, at least, a double standard. Students were too priggish to record sexual matters even in their personal diaries. Apparently relations between male students and "nice" girls on campus or in town were platonic, but lower-class girls were considered fair game.

Religion and politics. Theocratic New England spawned

higher education in America, shaping the religious milieu in which students lived and studied for more than two hundred years. Like many colleges to follow, Harvard was established "dreading to leave an illiterate Ministry to the Churches, when our present Ministers shall lie in the Dust."[4]

Although early higher education acted as a source of future ministers, the regimen of campus life did not produce a pious attitude. Hostility toward enforced religious practice was not an expression of religious radicalism or atheism, but a predictable resentment toward the burdensome restrictions placed upon students.

The students did not reject the religion which fostered such a constricting atmosphere, but they did rebel at the endless sermons and countless rules designed to ensure "cleanliness of thought." A vicious circle ensued in which faculty interpreted any dissension as evidence that students were in Satan's grip, requiring another round of sermons and sanctions in the never-ceasing struggle to save students from moral depravity.

Student piety did not interfere with their considerably high spirits. Nonetheless, religious orthodoxy prevailed. After all, most of the young scholars were aspirant ministers. Such orthodoxy had been threatened after the American Revolution when deism held sway and the ideology of the French Revolution captured youthful imaginations. But this era of skepticism was quickly swept away in the Great Revival during the first decade of the nineteenth century. Religious fervor inspired the establishment of the great denominational colleges in the new West. Revival meetings were held on many campuses, and students were "saved" en masse. Temperance leagues sprang up and were about as successful in eliminating intoxication on campus as they were in the general community.

Few students could distinguish between religious and political issues, for the dramatically moral overtones of national policy were enthusiastically grasped while the subtle nuances of cynical politicking were ignored. No issue was more dramatically moral than slavery. Campuses were rocked by angry abolitionists and antiabolitionists, with faculty frequently drawn into the debate. At Oberlin, abolition became a religious commitment, and militant students were actively involved in transporting slaves to freedom via the underground railroad.

In the years between the Revolution and the Civil War, fiercely

[4] "New England's First Fruits, 1643," in *ibid.*, p. 6.

nationalistic Americans discussed political issues with earnestness and passion, and no doubt collegians were no strangers to hot political argument. Unfortunately the record provides little insight into the emotions which moved students to laud or denounce the movements which defined the era. Nonetheless, the campus helped to shape many Northerners and Southerners, conservatives and liberals.

Prospects and expectations. Professors may sigh for a golden past in which students and administrators did not conceive of the total college experience as one grand rite of passage for full admission into the occupational arena. Such professorial nostalgia is for a time that never was. Since the founding of Harvard, "wherein a succession of a learned and able Ministry might be educated," American higher education has consistently been occupationally oriented. This theme has not always been specifically and intentionally expressed in the curriculum, but it is evident in the way the education has been utilized by graduates.

For example, the classical curriculum, emphasizing ancient languages, rhetoric, and classic moral philosophy, was obviously not designed to develop the skills demanded of ministerial leaders. There was certainly no attempt to foster within the curriculum itself specific prescriptions for vocational success in the ecclesiastical field, or in any other occupation. Nevertheless, this tradition-worshipping curriculum was a very useful device for clerical candidates, if only as a status symbol. In a new society, education itself was the mark of a "superior" man. Who could doubt the leadership capabilities of a man who could speak Greek?

So, at a very early date, the curriculum became subtly occupation-oriented, either by design or default. Specific prescriptions for occupational performance were not furnished by the curriculum, but the attributes of occupational status were imparted. Early in the nineteenth century the ever-perceptive de Tocqueville observed that in America

> . . . education ends at the age where [French] education begins. Whatever is done afterwards is with a view to some special and lucrative object; a science is taken up as a matter of business, and the only branch of it which is attended to is such as admits of an immediate practical application.[5]

Thus, the young man went to college to become a minister; he might eventually become something else, but chances were good that

---

[5] Alexis de Tocqueville, *Democracy in America,* edited and abridged by Richard Heffner (New York: Mentor Books, 1956), p. 53.

he was destined for a leadership role in the growing society. Usually, he had been recruited from among the elite, and obtained in college the properties and bearing with which he perpetuated his membership in that elite.

This is not to say every student was born with a silver spoon in his mouth that was to be polished in college until it glistened with wisdom. There were, in fact, those struggling students—so popular in fiction—who strove to attain an education which would move them up the rungs of the social ladder. Social acceptance of summer jobs was assured early in the emerging campus culture by the number of farmers' sons who entered college to acquire the means to win fame and fortune.

Higher Education in The New Society

America's growth proceeded in fits and spurts. One of the "spurts" was of particular importance to higher education. Mid-nineteenth century America moved rapidly from a pastoral to an urban society. Migration to the growing metropolises gave rise to an urban way of life, characterized by a depersonalization of social contacts.[6]

The emerging technology was accompanied by a burgeoning growth of corporate structures to manage and finance the sprawling enterprises fostered by industrialism. Land barons became (or were replaced by) industrial magnates; farmers became wage-earners.

Increasing specialization meant the creation of new roles and of new values to mediate the resultingly complex interrelationships among these roles.

The sweeping changes in American life introduced in the nineteenth century could be cataloged indefinitely. Dreiser, Steffens, and Sinclair knew well the social consequences of these changes. The generalizations to be lifted out of this tide of change spell a growing dependency upon bureaucracy—not only within business, but in all phases of American life.

This bureaucratization, and all the other changes which accompanied the rapid industrialization of America, had an effect on the attitudes and behavior of college students.

The new campus. The picture of early American campuses

---

[6] Louis Wirth, "Urbanism as a Way of Life," *American Journal of Sociology*, XLIV (1938–39), 1–24. George Simmel, "The Metropolis and Mental Life," in C. Wright Mills, *Images of Man* (New York: George Braziller, Inc., 1960), pp. 437–48.

presented thus far has particular relevance for the two hundred years from the founding of Harvard to the Civil War. Within that long period there were, of course, many modifications upon the themes noted. Also, many colleges retained characteristics of early campuses long after Appomattox. For instance, the classic curriculum did not disappear universally overnight. But no historian can help but be impressed by the raft of innovations introduced on campuses in the mid-nineteenth century.

First, American educators became intrigued with the German university system, and turned from the Oxford-Cambridge model. As adapted in America, the German university provided for the housing of technical, professional, research, and training facilities on the same campuses as traditional classical studies (which evolved into the liberal arts).

Second, large cracks appeared in the stolid wall of the classical curriculum, and in flooded the new sciences, along with a new pedagogy.

Third, a new and older breed of students appeared. By the 1880's college "boys" were described as college "men." The increasing numbers of women students added a genteel touch to campus culture. The new students saw the world and their studies differently, and formed different associations.

Fourth, campuses took on a new and prosperous atmosphere as psuedo-Gothic "cathedrals" (symbol of campus life for a generation of Hollywood movie fans) sprang up to shelter liberally endowed experiments and projects. Spurring this growth were new college revenue sources from both private and public funds. Reliance upon tuition, denominational support, and occasional gifts would never have made possible the academic colossus which has arisen in this past one hundred years.

Most striking were the huge personal donations of industrial entrepreneurs, and the federal support provided through land-grant colleges. The University of Chicago and Stanford University are examples of schools established through academic philanthropy, but they were part of a larger trend in which each school had—or sought—a voluntary benefactor among alumni and/or local business leaders.

Industry was not alone in shaping the direction of modern higher education. The great land-grant universities of the West and Midwest, established with public funds, were directly charged with an immediate and practical mission as training institutions in "mechanical and agricultural sciences" for "industrial classes." In these institutions, liberal and professional education has grown apace with applied sciences, but almost always as a supplement to a basically vocational program. In some cases (e.g., Cornell University and the University of Minnesota), private endowment combined with land-grant funds for development of strong universities with both vocational and research emphases.

Money proffered by beneficent legislatures and enlightened barons of industry did not come without strings—and, frequently, sturdy ropes—attached:

> Thus began a process which at most colleges eventually relegated the humanities to the dusty back rooms of Old Main while the sciences moved into million-dollar laboratory buildings, and the schools of business became the largest divisions of universities.[7]

But if industry bears the blame for commercialism on campus, it must also receive plaudits for furnishing much of the initiative for revitalizing the curriculum, and later the wherewithal for important basic research.

Fifth, the new higher education became more of an integral part of American society, serving a much larger public through a diversification of programs ranging from junior colleges and normal schools to professional and graduate schools.

Sixth, a whole roster of new roles appeared on campus. The simple division of labor between faculty and students proliferated into a complex of specialities. With the coming of the university, faculty responsibilities involved less policy-making and discipline and more research and instruction. College administration became a significant operation within itself, carrying the business ethic into the management of expanding campuses. Thorstein Veblen caustically observed:

> . . . introduction of business principles into university policy has had the ubiquitous effect of greatly heightening the directorate's solicitude for a due and creditable publicity, a convincing visible success, a tactful and effectual showing of efficiency reflected in an uninterrupted growth in size and other tangible quantitative features.[8]

In Veblen's time, this administration was frequently consolidated in the office of the president, a position which grew enormously

---

[7] Earnest, *op. cit.,* p. 140.

[8] Thorstein Veblen, *The Higher Learning in America* (Stanford, Calif.: Academic Reprints, 1954), p. 135.

from that of senior instructor maintaining liaison between fellow staff members and the governing board. Since Veblen wrote, university administrations have tended to evolve from omnipotent presidencies into a system of committees, business and public relations agents, experts in management and personnel, and so on.

As in any historical development, all these factors of change in higher education had interacting sources and interlocking results. Abandonment of drill and recitation (instructional methods which accompanied the classical curriculum) was fostered by the expanding school population, which made such methods no longer feasible. Lectures, demonstrations, and eventually experiments were found to be more amenable in transmitting the new knowledge of the age of Darwin. The growing maturity of students was related to the introduction of public high schools, co-education, and, initially, to the influx of Civil War veterans earnestly desiring training prepatory to making as much money as possible. And they were more likely to find what they wanted as endowments were offered for programs that would help industry restock its firms with young blood. Of course, enrollment growth contributed directly to the bureaucratization of campus administration.

This bureaucratization was to play a significant role in altering the character and attitudes of students. As universities emerged as young giants in newly industrialized America, students found that the depersonalization which resulted from the rationally derived complex social structures of their home communities was reflected on the campus. Thus, the "campus way of life" emerged, with its own styles of existence devoid of the specific business of the university, just as the "urban way of life" has little relationship to specific career motifs.

All these processes of change in the formal structure of universities and in the informal campus culture, along with changes in the traditions inherited from earlier American colleges, combined to produce a unique association for higher learning in this country quite unlike its predecessors here or abroad.

The College Student in Industrial America

Campus life and campus groups. Debate societies gave way to the fraternity system, which was to dominate social life on many campuses for the century after the Civil War. The first fraternities were founded in the 1830's and 1840's, but not until some thirty years later did they supplant debate societies on many campuses. These debate societies died out for lack of any meaningful function: oratory for its own sake became less popular in this more sophisticated era, and skills of argumentation and elocution were more effectively transmitted through classroom speech and forensics programs.

With the disappearance of debate societies, fraternities filled a social gap not bridged either by classes or by the common experience of the classroom. The class was no longer a manageable unit for social interaction; its significance was reduced to junior proms, election of popular collegiates as class officers, and the like.

The classroom really no longer provided a common experience, for the elective system created a diffusion of interests among students. An increasing specialization in the American job hierarchy resulted in a corresponding specialization within the academic curricula. A junior majoring in entomology was totally indifferent to the academic concerns of his peers studying English history.

Then, too, Americans increasingly resented an intrusion of work ethic or activities into their leisure worlds.[9] This bifurcation of life motifs between work and leisure contributed to the failure of American students to form permanent social bonds through their studies. This distinct compartmentalization of campus life is reflected in student hostility toward the suggestion that tutors live in fraternity houses to provide academic assistance after school hours.

The conviviality of the fraternity system met an institutional need within the growingly complex social structure of the campus to find some equivalent to the family associations available in the larger community. Just as families sometimes found themselves at odds with bureaucratic structures in modern industrial America, the norms and values of fraternities were at times quite independent of the official norms and values of colleges.

With fraternities came sharper social class distinctions, especially in the older schools of the East. As institutions mature within a maturing social order, those symbols which distinguish members of various social classes become more exclusive, and channels for social class interaction and mobility are more rigidly defined. This process is evident in the history of American campus life. The latter part of the nineteenth century saw the sons of Veblen's leisure class very

---

[9] C. Wright Mills, *White Collar* (New York: Oxford University Press, Inc., 1956), pp. 235–38.

conspicuously consuming in the elite clubs and fraternities of the East.

The prototype of the modern student in the Golden Era of business growth was one quite intent upon occupational success. But that does not necessarily imply he was a serious student. The socialite participating in what Woodrow Wilson termed the "sideshow" on campus, and not the scholar, became hero of campus life. The "gentlemen's C" was the norm. In fact, student norms called for going out of the way to avoid the epithet of *scholar* or *intellectual*. Editorship of the school paper, high office in a prestigious fraternity, athletic prowess—these meant a successful campus career.

In this aura, sports became an unweildy giant on college campuses. To many Americans, the most familiar college official was the ticket-seller at football games. Through the years controversy waged among college spokesmen and in the popular press regarding commercial exploitation of college football.

The emphasis football received at the turn of the century was largely supported by the nonplaying student body. "We toil not, neither do we agitate, but we play football" was the boast of the Yale class of 1901. Students have seemed indifferent to the controversy over the "capture" of college sports by commercial interests, nor have they audibly endorsed or denounced the morality of a sport claimed to injure combatants seriously. Students passively supported football and contributed to the colorful holiday atmosphere of football weekends. Glamor and excitement formerly enlivening festive commencement celebrations now engulfed these marketable sporting rituals.

Manners and morals. The taming of the West coincided with the taming of college students. The students of sixty years ago may have been carefree and happy-go-lucky, but they certainly were not the riotous drunkards who had torn up the town in earlier decades. Drinking was much less a problem than it had been previously, and faculties found it less necessary to teach with one hand while brandishing weapons with the other.[10]

During the post-Civil War era, the "natural" conflict between faculty and students was intensified by their differences over the fraternity system. Faculties believed that, out of loyalty to their fraternities, students would deceive to protect fellow brothers. But as fraternities begat successful and influential alumni, the fraternity

---

[10] Charles Thwing, *American Colleges* (New York: G. P. Putnam's Sons, 1883), p. 40.

question was settled for all time, and student-faculty relations settled into an institutionalized mutual distrust characterized by benign wariness and suspicion.

Some of this distruct was generated by the propensity of students to cheat in recitation and examination. Students suffered little remorse in referring to shirt cuffs and ponies for information they doubted had any future usefulness. The reforms which marked this era were slow in coming; meanwhile, student moral responsibility languished wherever the classical curricula went grinding on. However, the same moral code which condoned ingenious cribbing brought forth its most powerful sanctions upon the collegiate who failed in his fraternity obligations.

Men and women. As suffragettes in bloomers marched in waves down Main Street demanding the right to vote, their younger sisters were marching into classrooms to demand a college education. Coeducation was an accepted practice in the large state universities blossoming over the West. The Victorian notion of feminine fragility and fraility was a barrier to women who sought an equal opportunity for exposure to a variety of educational programs. Even after women had proven their stamina in successful classroom competition with men (and not infrequently out-conjugating the men at their own Greek games), some felt a necessity to discuss the physical capacity of women for higher education.[11]

After the emergence of the modern college man in the latter half of the 1800's, nothing altered the character of campus life so much as the changes in role expectations of and for women students. The same Victorian ideal which saw women as frail and fragile sought to keep them that way. If college girls were not keepers of the home fires, they were supposed to be keepers of all that was "chaste" and "pure." It fell upon women destined to be housewives or schoolmarms to uphold the virtues of the innocent life. And uphold them they did.

It was the change in these feminine roles, argues Ernest Earnest, which really gave college youth of the Roaring Twenties their label as the grand campus hellians of all time. The gay young blade of the Gay Nineties campus was quite literally father to his son, the flaming youth of the 1920's. But the flapper daughter bore little resemblance to her prim Victorian mother, who had married the gay young blade. The aggressive self-emancipation of women con-

---

[11] *Ibid.,* pp. 178–200.

tributed to the rebellious nature of the post-World War I decade.[12]

Relationships between the sexes altered with this changing pattern. The double standard traditionally applied to sexual behavior noted in earlier times was well institutionalized by the 1880's. Only with the 1920's did a more liberal mode emerge. Until after World War II, student marriages were rare, and officially prohibited by most colleges.

Religion and politics.   Industrialization in America was accompanied by secularization of the moral order. Religion, like leisure, became a compartmentalized facet of American life, isolated from everyday concerns and decisions of the mill and marketplace. The turn-of-the-century-campus hero of the fraternity and football set was not irreligious; but he did not permit religion—or much of anything else—to spoil his fun. He was not a deep thinker on religious, political, or economic issues. For him, these concerns simply did not exist, for the campuses of that era existed in isolation from the social problems which inflamed populists, muckrakers, and the new novelists.

Of course this picture of the typical student in the typical institution has been painted with very broad strokes. A tremendous diversity of institutional types developed and, within them, any number of personality types. Obviously not every collegian was a buddy of Frank Merriwell.

In the West and the South, areas still largely rural, religion remained the *raison d'être* for many colleges and their students. Many of these smaller schools, supported by a variety of religious denominations, are reminiscent of Eastern colleges in their earliest period of growth. Piety was the primary code of thought and action for students of the colleges which flourished in the Bible belt. Such schools have continued, if in a less predominant status, to this day.

Eastern universities furnished the stereotype out of which American journalists have created the image of the campus as hotbeds of radical agnosticism or outright atheism. The closest atheism ever really came to becoming campus religion was during the iconoclastic 1920's and the depressed and depressing 1930's. For the larger part, religion has not been absent from campus; rather, as in the families and communities of industrial America, it was given a specific time and place outside the routine of everyday concerns.

Student interest in national politics has paralleled the country's

---

[12] Robert Cooley Angell, *The Campus* (New York: Appleton-Century-Crofts, 1928), pp. 12–34.

fortunes—rising in times of national crisis, and diminishing to the point of absence in such quiescent times as the pre-World War I decades. As students were pricked by social and intellectual revolutions of the 1920's and 1930's, they took a more vibrant role in American political life. Just as the slavery issue mobilized student concern in the previous century, the drama and controversy of depression economics invigorated campus thinking and action. Again the more extreme positions of conservative or liberal, Right or Left, attracted student enthusiasm.[13] Meanwhile, local campus politics received attention in inverse relationship to involvement in national politics. For example, student political affairs received primary priority in those very years before World War I when national and international issues lay relatively dormant.

Prospects and expectations.   The heroes of preindustrial America ventured to college and returned home as ministers, lawyers, or teachers. They were professional men; few other fields required such education.

The heroes of more recent times went to college, the university, the community college, the technical institute, the normal school, or some other institution of higher education, and became bank managers, engineers, social workers, farmers, and so on. Jobs previously requiring no higher education now made such experience mandatory; jobs never existing in man's imagination before the industrial age now called for expertise requiring years of training.

Expansion of the little army of students recruited by the professions began with the enlistment of graduates by the business community. In the simpler era of fifty years ago, fraternity contacts sufficed to insure a berth on Wall Street or in a law firm. With the sophistication of academic allocative functions, eager undergraduates now are screened, tested, ranked, priced, and marketed by colleges and universities.

Higher education is no longer peculiar to the professional elite. In terms of economics, the academic degree may mark the "consuming" elite of today; but higher education is to some degree common both to political elite and to proletariat.

---

[13] James Wechsler, *Revolt on Campus* (New York: Covici, Friede, 1935), *passim.*

Social Structure, Social Change, and the College Student

Social structure is the fabric of an institution, woven out of common expectations for behavior specific to that institution. Social structure also includes functioning roles within an institution, either in their vertical (hierarchical) arrangement or in their horizontal interaction for performance of institutional tasks. Through such aspects of social structure as common expectations and roles, some characteristics of evolving student personality have been surmised.

Mutual articulation of culture and personality is a familiar problem to sociologists and anthropologists. Within the context of that concern, changing campus social structure can be seen as generating, and being generated by, appropriate personality adaptations.

Furthermore, this changing campus social structure has been cast with particular reference to change in the larger social order. Sociologists have offered typologies expressing diverse but overlapping facets of this variation in social arrangements. Thus society and/or culture may be folk or urban, *gemeinschaft* or *gesellschaft,* mechanic or organic in solidarity, sacred or secular, and so on. All these dichotomies represent extreme ends of continua characterized by variation from simple-to-complex interaction patterns, homogeneous-to-heterogeneous organizational units, and/or personal-to-corporate contacts.[14]

Campus culture, when viewed before and after the industrialization of America, is an example of such proliferation of social structure. Such significant shifts in social structure as occurred in America, and on campus, imply corresponding shifts in personality and character motifs.

The pious (but rebellious) youngster whiling away the time in a colonial college is not of the same personality as the impious hedonist who occupied campus a century later—largely because the college social structure which made each of these fellows changed from folk to urban, from *gemeinschaft* to *gesellschaft,* from sacred to secular.

---

[14] John McKinney and Charles Loomis, "The Typological Tradition," in Joseph Roucek, *Readings in Contemporary American Sociology* (Patterson, N.J.: Littlefield, Adams, 1961), pp. 557–82.

CHAPTER III

The Changing College Student Population

JOHN FRED THADEN

Professor Emeritus, Sociology
Demographer, Institute
for Community Development

The postwar baby boom foretells that the remaining years of this decade and most of the 1970's will go down in history as the period of the college enrollment explosion. During the fourteen-year period, 1946–59, a total of 55 million babies were born in this country, in contrast to only 36 million during the preceding fourteen year period. The recently rising trends in college enrollment have been small ripples in comparison to the tidal wave that will roll from now on until about 1980.

The rapidly increasing college-age population will be accentuated by at least two socioeducational phenomena. One is the ever-increasing proportion of persons of nearly all ages pursuing higher education; the other is the gradual rise in the educational level of adults. Educated parents tend to have high educational expectations of their children. The interrelationship of these phenomena and related factors merit consideration and constitute the essential substance of this chapter.

Trends in College-Age Population

The age range of college students gradually increases. Today college students constitute a much wider range than the ages eighteen to twenty-one. The actual span ranges from as young as fifteen to persons of retirement age. According to the U.S. Census Bureau, a total of 2.2 million persons eighteen to twenty-four years of age were enrolled in college in 1960. In addition, 656,000 persons age twenty-five to thirty-four, and a large but unknown number of persons thirty-five years of age and over, were also attending college. Throughout this chapter "college-age" will pertain primarily to eighteen to twenty-four years of age.

Trends since 1910. In general, the total population has been increasing more rapidly than the college-age (eighteen to twenty-four) population because of the more rapid growth of the older age segments. Decreasing death rates and increasing longevity have been important contributing factors to this pattern.

Table 1 shows that the total population of United States increased gradually from 92 million in 1910 to 179 million in 1960. During the same half-century, the college-age population increased irregularly from 12.7 million in 1910 to 15.6 million in 1960. During the fifty-year period, total population increased 95 per cent while the college-age population increased only 22 per cent. The declining birth rate during the 1920's and 1930's was to affect the number of late teen-agers some two decades later. It will be noted that there were 229,000 fewer persons eighteen to twenty-four years of age in 1960 than in 1950, and this reflects the comparatively lower birth rate of two decades earlier.

Decennial changes in total population do not necessarily reflect direction or relative change in college-age population. From 1910 to 1920, the total population of the United States increased 14.9 per cent while the college-age population increased only 2.1 per cent. During the 1920's, the total population increased 16.1 per cent while the college-age population increased even more (18.8 per cent). During the 1930's, the trends were reversed: the total population increased 7.2 per cent while the college-age population decreased 7.4 per cent. During the 1940's, the trends were similiar: the total population increased somewhat more rapidly than the college-age population (14.5 and 10.5 per cent, respectively). The decade 1950–60 exhibits a most unusual inverse relationship: the total population increased 19.0 per cent while the college-age population decreased 1.4 per cent. This reflects the effects of the relatively few births during the depression years.

The college-age segment comprised 13.9 per cent of the total population in 1910. This percentage gradually decreased; it was down to 8.7 in 1960. This trend will be reversed during the next few decades. The present 15.6 million persons eighteen to twenty-four years of age will be replaced in 1970 by the survivors, plus some immigrants, of the 23.9 million children who are presently eight to fourteen years of age. The census of 1970 may reveal approximately 8 million more college-age persons in the nation than in 1960; it is estimated that they may then comprise about 12 per cent of the total population.

TABLE 1

TOTAL AND COLLEGE-AGE POPULATION: 1910–60

Year	TOTAL POPULATION		COLLEGE-AGE POPULATION		
	Number	Per cent Change	Number	Per cent Change	Per cent of total population
1910	91,972,266	—	12,748,411	—	13.9
1920	105,710,620	14.9	13,018,001	2.1	12.3
1930	122,775,046	16.1	15,463,657	18.8	12.6
1940	131,669,275	7.2	14,325,610	—7.4	10.9
1950	150,697,361	14.5	15,832,855	10.5	10.5
1960	179,323,175	19.0	15,604,167	—1.4	8.7

Source: U.S. Bureau of the Census, *U.S. Census of Population: 1960.* Vol. 1, *Characteristics of the Population,* Part 1, United States Summary, Tables 2, 46, and 47; also earlier censuses. The 1960 figures include Alaska and Hawaii.

Trends by sex. Females of college age are increasing faster than males. This is to be expected, for it is also the trend in the total population. Table 2 shows trends in the number of college-age males and females in the United States, by decades, since 1910. Males totaled 6.4 million in 1910; they were 19.1 per cent more numerous in 1960, but they were less numerous in 1960 than in 1950 or 1940 and reflect the dropping birth rates of the 1920's and 1930's. Despite recent declines in the number of college-age males, there has been an increase in college enrollment of males.

In general, the trend in the number of college-age females parallels that of the college-age males. However, college-age females increased from 6.3 million in 1910 to 7.9 million in 1960, a rise of 25.7 per cent. Females of college-age were less numerous than males of the same age in 1910, but they have outnumbered males since.

TABLE 2

COLLEGE-AGE POPULATION BY SEX: 1910–60

Year	Males		Females		Sex ratio (males per 1000 females)
	Number	Per cent change	Number	Per cent change	
1910	6,419,000	—	6,329,000	—	1,014
1920	6,372,000	—0.7	6,646,000	5.0	959
1930	7,601,000	19.3	7,863,000	18.3	967
1940	8,188,000	7.7	8,419,000	7.1	973
1950	7,783,000	—4.7	8,108,000	—3.7	960
1960	7,648,000	—1.7	7,956,000	—1.9	961
1910–60	1,229,000	19.1	1,629,000	25.7	

Source: U.S. Bureau of the Census, *U.S. Census of Population: 1960.* Vol. 1, *Characteristics of the Population,* Part 1, United States Summary, Tables 46 and 47; also earlier censuses. The 1960 figures include Alaska and Hawaii.

Presently, college-age girls outnumber the men by 326,000. Because of the increasing longevity of women, compared with men, the difference can be expected to grow larger.

The sex ratio by decades is also presented in Table 2. In general, the numerical predominance of women in recent decades reflects their lower death rates for at birth males outnumber females by about 1056 to 1000. Presently, the imbalance is small at eighteen years of age (996), greater at nineteen years of age (961), and greatest at twenty to twenty-four years of age (1954). Part of the disparity at present and in 1950 must be attributed to the exclusion from the census count of persons in the armed services abroad.

Table 3 indicates the number of people in the United States in 1960, eighteen to thirty-four years of age, by sex. There are over 2 million in each single year. The eighteen-year-olds are the most numerous (2.5 million). There is a total of 15,577,702 in the age group eighteen to twenty-four.

TABLE 3

POPULATION, EIGHTEEN–THIRTY-FOUR YEARS OF AGE, BY SEX: 1960

Age	Total	Male	Female	Per cent females outnumber males
18	2,498,600	1,249,225	1,249,375	.01
19	2,275,937	1,107,977	1,167,960	5.41
20	2,190,081	1,065,814	1,124,267	5.48
21	2,203,165	1,083,261	1,119,904	3.38
22	2,158,805	1,060,321	1,098,484	3.60
23	2,106,815	1,033,690	1,073,125	3.81
24	2,144,299	1,040,142	1,104,157	6.15
18–19	4,774,537	2,357,202	2,417,335	2.55
20–24	10,803,165	5,283,228	5,519,937	4.48
18–24	15,577,702	7,640,430	7,937,272	3.89
25–29	10,870,386	5,333,282	5,537,104	3.82
30–34	11,951,709	5,840,287	6,111,422	4.64

Source: U.S. Bureau of the Census, U.S. Census of Population: 1960. Vol. 1, Part 1, United States Summary, Tables 155 and 156.

Females outnumber the males at all ages—by a very narrow margin at age eighteen and by the widest margin (6.2 per cent) at age twenty-four. In the eighteen-to-twenty-four age group, there are 7,640,430 males and 7,937,272 females—a difference of 296,842, or 3.9 per cent.

Those twenty to twenty-four years of age are slightly less numerous than those twenty-five to twenty-nine and substantially fewer than those thirty to thirty-four years of age and reflect the difference in birth rates during the so-called prosperous 1920's and the depression 1930's.

Females outnumber males at ages twenty-five to twenty-nine by 203,822 persons and at ages thirty to thirty-four by 271,135 persons, which indicates the higher survival rates of females.

Trend in color and racial composition. Population may be classified as white and nonwhite. Of the total college-age population in 1960, 13.7 million (87.8 per cent) were white and 1.9 million (12.2 per cent) were nonwhite. Since 1950, the white population in this age group decreased by 376,000 while the nonwhite group increased by 54,000. Most of the nonwhite population is Negro (92 per cent), and the rest (8 per cent) is composed of Indians, Japanese, Chinese, and Filipinos.

Trends in rural-urban composition. The population of the United States has been predominantly urban since 1920. Presently, 11 million persons of the college-age population are urban and 4.5 million are rural. Since 1950, the urban population in this age group increased 4.7 per cent and the rural population decreased 16.6 per cent.

The rural population is commonly divided into nonfarm and farm subclasses. At present, of the college-age population, the rural nonfarm category comprises 3.6 million and the rural farm category comprises only 946,000. The nonfarm population of college age is increasing while the rural farm population is decreasing.

Trends in College Enrollment

Resident degree-credit college enrollment in the United States increased from 355,213 in 1909–10 to 3.3 million in 1957–58, according to the U.S. Office of Education, as disclosed in Table 4. These figures include both full-time and part-time resident students in 1940 institutions of higher education. They do not include extension students and summer-session enrollments. The 1957–58 enrollment was nearly triple that of 1929–30, while total population increased only about 41 per cent.

Resident degree-credit college enrollment may be computed as a ratio of the total college-age population, which increased from 2.9 per cent in 1909–10 to 21.4 per cent in 1957–58. The increase was considerable each decade. Presently, the ratio may already be one to four.

Since 1909–10, undergraduate enrollment increased from 346,-060 to 2.9 million in 1957–58, more than an eight fold increase. During the same period, graduate enrollment increased from 9153 to 344,647—a thirty-seven fold increase.

In 1909–10 and 1919–20, graduate students comprised 2.6 per cent of the total resident degree-credit enrollment. This had increased to 10.5 per cent by 1957–58. Graduate students are normally twenty-two years of age and older, while a considerable proportion of undergraduates are still in their teens.

The plan for future college enrollment surveys by the U.S. Office of Education is to emphasize enrollment for the fall term only. Such data will vary somewhat from academic-year data by virtue of late enrollments and dropouts.

In a sense, the data in Table 4 is brought up to date by stating that the total degree-credit enrollment increased from 3,068,417 in the fall of 1957 to 4,988,000 in the fall of 1964.

TABLE 4

RESIDENT DEGREE-CREDIT COLLEGE ENROLLMENT, SINCE 1909–10

| | —TOTAL ENROLLMENT— | | | | Graduates |
Year	Number	Ratio of Population 18–24 %	Under-graduate	Number	% of total enrollment
1909–10	355,213	2.9	346,060	9,153	2.6
1919–20	597,880	4.7	582,268	15,612	2.6
1929–30	1,110,737	7.2	1,053,482	47,255	4.3
1939–40	1,494,203	9.1	1,388,456	105,748	7.1
1949–50	2,659,021	16.5	2,421,813	237,208	8.9
1957–58	3,283,917	21.4	2,939,270	344,647	10.5

Source: U.S. Department of Health, Education, and Welfare, *Biennial Survey of Education in the United States, Statistics of Higher Education 1957–58, 1962,* Table 3.

Trends by age. The U.S. Census Bureau reports 2.9 million persons age fifteen to thirty-four enrolled in college in 1960. How many thousands, age thirty-five and over, are enrolled in college is not indicated in published census reports. Table 5 discloses the number and percentage of people eighteen to thirty-four years of age enrolled in elementary schools, high schools, and colleges. A majority of eighteen-year-olds, 30.1 per cent, are still in high school and 1.7 per cent are still in elementary school; nearly one-fifth, 18.8 per cent, are in college. As one would expect, at successively higher ages, the proportion enrolled in elementary school and in high school tends to decrease and the proportion enrolled in college tends to increase.

The Census Bureau reports 1803 persons age fifteen in college, 6492 age sixteen, and 56,276 age seventeen. In fact 2 per cent of those age seventeen are in college. However, for practical purposes, analysis of college enrollment trends is best depicted by showing those eighteen years of age and over.

TABLE 5

POPULATION EIGHTEEN TO THIRTY-FOUR YEARS OF AGE ENROLLED IN
SCHOOL AND COLLEGE, BY AGE: 1960

Age	Total Population	Elementary School	High School	College
18	2,498,600	42,370	752,656	469,172
19	2,275,937	31,301	201,853	512,089
20	2,190,081	15,150	88,759	410,331
21	2,203,165	12,995	65,560	333,256
22	2,158,805	11,324	45,733	211,977
23	2,106,815	14,716	39,774	149,513
24	2,144,299	9,673	41,074	128,176
18–24	15,577,702	137,529	1,235,409	2,214,514
25–29	10,870,386	41,653	175,300	445,786
30–34	11,951,709	44,334	124,312	210,575
		PER CENT		
18	100.0	1.7	30.1	18.8
19	100.0	1.3	8.9	22.5
20	100.0	0.7	4.1	18.7
21	100.0	0.6	3.0	15.1
22	100.0	0.5	2.1	9.8
23	100.0	0.7	1.9	7.1
24	100.0	0.4	1.7	6.0
18–24	100.0	0.9	7.9	14.2
25–29	100.0	0.4	1.6	4.1
30–34	100.0	0.4	1.0	1.8

Source: U.S. Bureau of the Census, *U.S. Census of Population: 1960.* Vol. 1, Part 1, United States Summary, Table 168.

More college students are nineteen years of age than any other age. They are trailed by those eighteen years of age, followed in order by those age twenty, twenty-one, twenty-two, and so on.

A significantly higher proportion of nineteen-year-olds are enrolled in college than of any other age group: 22.5 per cent. Some 18.8 per cent of the eighteen-year-olds are in college, followed by 18.7 per cent of the twenty-year-olds, 15.1 per cent of the twenty-one-year-olds, and less than 10 per cent of those twenty-two, twenty-three, and twenty-four years of age. One person in seven of eighteen to twenty-four years of age is enrolled in college. A significant proportion (4.1 per cent) of those twenty-five to twenty-nine years of age are enrolled, and 1.8 per cent of those thirty to thirty-four years of age.

Changes in college enrollment.   The U.S. Census Bureau reveals that in 1950 a total of nearly 1.7 million people eighteen to twenty-four years of age were enrolled in college. By 1960 this figure had increased to 2.2 million, as indicated in Table 6. In 1950 10.6 per cent of the college-age population were enrolled. This had increased to 14.2 per cent by 1960. This figure may increase to 18 per cent by 1970. The rise in college enrollment of those twenty-five to twenty-nine years of age from 3.7 per cent in 1950 to 4.1 per cent in 1960 is also significant.

TABLE 6

POPULATION EIGHTEEN TO THIRTY-FOUR YEARS OF AGE ENROLLED IN COLLEGE, BY AGE: 1950 AND 1960

Age	NUMBER		PER CENT	
	1950	1960	1950	1960
18	265,985	469,172	17.2	18.8
19	334,965	512,089	20.8	22.5
20	291,900	410,331	17.6	18.7
21	255,455	333,256	14.6	15.1
22	203,380	211,977	11.5	9.8
23	170,540	149,513	9.4	7.1
24	143,300	128,176	7.8	6.0
18–24	1,665,525	2,214,514	10.6	14.2
25–29	447,200	445,786	3.7	4.1
30–34	n.a.	210,575	—	1.8

Source: U.S. Bureau of the Census, *U.S. Census of Population: 1960.* Vol. 1, Part 1, Tables 155 and 168. Also, *U.S. Census of Population: 1950, Vol. II: Characteristics of the Population, Part 1: U.S. Summary,* Chap. C, Tables 94 and 112.

Evidently, there is a growing tendency to pursue collegiate studies soon after high school graduation. This is shown by the higher proportion of persons in their late teens and early twenties who are in college now as compared to 1950. College enrollment of eighteen-year-olds rose from 17.2 per cent to 18.8 per cent; of nineteen-year-olds from 20.8 to 22.5 per cent; of twenty-year-olds from 17.6 to 18.7 per cent; and of twenty-one-year-olds from 14.6 to 15.1 per cent.

College enrollment increases during the 1960's may closely resemble that of the 1950's in view of increasing demand for college-trained men. It is possible that 25 per cent of the nineteen-year-olds and 20 per cent of the eighteen- and twenty-year-olds will be enrolled in college in 1970.

Trends by sex. Many forces exert pressure upon high school graduates to go to college and to do so immediately upon graduation, or soon afterwards. This explains the phenomenal increase between 1950 and 1960 in the proportion of both males and females, eighteen to twenty-four years of age, attending college, as portrayed in Table 7.

TABLE 7

POPULATION EIGHTEEN TO THIRTY-FOUR YEARS OF AGE ENROLLED IN
COLLEGE, BY SEX: 1950 AND 1960

| | NUMBER | | | | PER CENT | | | |
| | Males | | Females | | Males | | Females | |
Age	1950	1960	1950	1960	1950	1960	1950	1960
18	130,405	235,299	135,580	233,873	12.1	18.8	12.3	18.7
19	178,295	276,363	156,670	235,726	16.9	24.9	14.2	20.2
20	165,980	236,975	125,920	173,356	15.8	22.2	11.1	15.4
21	166,190	209,631	89,265	123,625	14.9	19.4	7.7	11.1
22	158,230	154,894	45,150	57,083	14.2	14.6	3.8	5.2
23	144,010	117,550	26,530	31,963	12.7	11.4	2.2	3.0
24	122,870	103,754	20,430	24,422	10.8	10.0	1.7	2.2
18–24	1,065,980	1,334,466	599,545	880,048	13.9	17.5	7.4	11.1
25–29	374,760	365,014	72,440	80,772	6.3	6.8	1.2	1.4
30–34	n.a.	148,743	n.a.	61,832	—	2.6	—	1.0

Source: U.S. Bureau of the Census, *U.S. Census of Population: 1960.* Vol. 1, Part 1, Table 168.

In 1950, a total of one million males in this age group were enrolled in college. By 1960, this figure had jumped to 1.3 million. In other words, the proportion rose from 13.9 per cent to 17.5 per cent. The demand for people with advanced schooling boosted the college enrollment of males from twenty-five to twenty-nine years of age from 6.3 to 6.8 per cent. The proportionate increase was largest for those eighteen years of age followed in turn by those at ages nineteen, twenty, and twenty-one.

There is a possibility that over 20 per cent of the males at ages eighteen to twenty-four will be in college by 1970. Already, 24.9 per cent of the nineteen-year-olds are enrolled and 22.2 per cent of the twenty-year-olds.

Presently, a larger proportion of males than of females at all ages is enrolled in college. The difference is insignificant at age eighteen. At age nineteen, one in four males and one in five females are enrolled. At age twenty, 22.2 per cent of the males and over 15.4 per cent of the females are enrolled. With increasing age the gap widens, at least during the principal child-bearing years. A much larger proportion of men than women pursue courses in graduate school so that at age twenty-four nearly five times as many men as women are in college (10.0 and 2.2 per cent, respectively).

At age eighteen, the tendency for girls to continue their education beyond high school is as strong as it is for boys of the same age. The tendency gradually weakens thereafter. For the eighteen-to-twenty-one age group, only 11.1 per cent of the girls are enrolled in college compared to 17.5 per cent of the males.

At all ages a much larger proportion of females were enrolled in college in 1960 than in 1950. This trend was strongest at age eighteen, when the percentage increased from 12.3 to 18.7. The trend was weakest for those twenty-four years of age and older. The proportion of college-age women enrolled in college will probably increase from the present 11.1 per cent to about 15 per cent by 1970.

Trends by color.   Over twice as large a proportion of the white as of the nonwhite college-age population are enrolled in college—15.2 per cent as compared to 7.0 per cent (see Table 8). The differential is greatest at age eighteen. One in five of the white persons at

TABLE 8

POPULATION EIGHTEEN TO THIRTY-FOUR YEARS OF AGE ENROLLED IN
COLLEGE, BY COLOR: 1950 AND 1960

	NUMBER				PER CENT			
	White		Nonwhite		White		Nonwhite	
Age	1950	1960	1950	1960	1950	1960	1950	1960
18	253,240	444,544	12,745	24,618	13.2	20.2	4.8	8.1
19	318,895	482,557	16,070	29,532	16.6	24.2	6.7	10.5
20	276,980	384,245	14,920	26,086	14.3	20.0	5.9	9.6
21	242,600	312,522	12,855	20,734	12.0	16.1	5.1	7.9
22	193,155	197,930	10,225	14,047	9.5	10.4	3.9	5.4
23	162,155	139,528	8,385	9,985	7.8	7.5	3.2	3.9
24	135,930	119,269	7,370	8,907	6.5	6.4	2.8	3.3
18–24	1,582,955	2,080,595	82,570	133,909	14.6	15.2	4.6	7.0
25–29	421,990	411,786	25,210	34,000	3.9	4.3	1.9	2.6
30–34	n.a.	193,069	n.a.	17,506	—	18.2	—	1.3

Source: U.S. Bureau of the Census, *U.S. Census of Population: 1960.* Vol. 1, Part 1, Table 168.

age eighteen are in college compared to only one in twelve of the nonwhite. The contrast is less at ages nineteen, twenty, and twenty-one. At ages twenty-two, twenty-three, and twenty-four, the proportion of whites attending college is less than twice as high as of nonwhites. In other words, nonwhite students are delayed in their entrance to college and therefore nonwhite college students tend to be older than their white classmates. In this connection, it may be remembered that 92 per cent of the nonwhite college-age population are Negroes.

The nonwhite population made greater advances in college attendance at all ages than the white population during the past decade. This was natural in view of the comparatively low position of the nonwhite population at the beginning of the period. Advancement among both whites and nonwhites was most pronounced at age eighteen and, in general, tended to decrease thereafter.

If the percentage of the nonwhite college-age population attending college in 1960 had been as high as for the white population (14.6 per cent), nonwhite enrollment would have been about 270,-300 instead of 133,909.

A continued rise in the proportion of population of most ages attending college seems inevitable and will be relatively more rapid among the nonwhite than among the white population for some time.

Trends in urban population. An increasing proportion of urban dwellers are going to college. The percentage of the college-age urban population enrolled in college in 1950 was 14.0, which had increased to 17.7 by 1960 (Table 9). The greatest relative increase occurred among the teen-agers. Of those eighteen years old, the percentage attending college increased from 17.2 to 24.0. College enrollment rose from 20.8 to 27.9 per cent among those nineteen years of age. There was a slight increase among those twenty-five to twenty-nine years of age, although it is still less than one in twenty.

Probably more than 20 per cent of college-age urban dwellers will be in college in 1970. It does not seem unreasonable to expect that approximately one of every three eighteen- and nineteen-year-old urban youths will be attending college in 1970 or soon thereafter.

It should be noted that the U.S. Census Bureau's figures on college enrollment of urban people contain many persons, especially farm people, whose residence normally is elsewhere. In both 1950 and 1960, for instance, college students were considered residents of the communities in which they were residing while attending college.

TABLE 9

URBAN POPULATION EIGHTEEN TO THIRTY-FOUR YEARS OF AGE ENROLLED
IN COLLEGE: 1950 AND 1960

Age	NUMBER		PER CENT	
	1950	1960	1950	1960
18	225,760	409,473	17.2	24.0
19	285,545	445,025	20.8	27.9
20	250,270	361,966	17.6	23.3
21	221,970	296,403	14.6	18.7
22	177,300	188,290	11.5	12.1
23	149,360	132,637	9.4	8.8
24	125,355	123,283	7.8	8.0
18–24	1,434,560	1,957,077	14.0	17.7
25–29	389,025	393,166	4.6	4.9
30–34	n.a.	180,648	—	2.1

Source: U.S. Bureau of the Census, *U.S. Census of Population: 1960.* Vol. 1, Part 1, Table 168.

Trends in rural nonfarm population. Table 10 indicates the number and percentage of rural nonfarm youths attending college in 1950 and 1960. In the college-age group the percentage rose from 5.6 to 9.2. At present, 10.8 per cent of the nineteen-year-olds are in college, followed by 8.6 per cent of the eighteen-year-olds, 8.3 per cent of the twenty-year-olds and gradually smaller percentages among those twenty-one to twenty-four years of age.

Over 47,000 rural nonfarm people, or nearly 2 per cent of those twenty-five to twenty-nine years of age, are enrolled in college, and

TABLE 10

RURAL NONFARM POPULATION EIGHTEEN TO THIRTY-FOUR YEARS OF AGE
ENROLLED IN COLLEGE: 1950 AND 1960

Age	NUMBER		PER CENT	
	1950	1960	1950	1960
18	16,040	50,287	6.5	8.6
19	23,020	56,874	8.6	10.8
20	20,330	41,649	7.0	8.3
21	18,700	32,283	5.9	6.5
22	17,020	20,886	4.6	4.2
23	15,225	15,165	3.8	3.0
24	13,120	13,507	3.2	2.7
18–24	123,455	230,651	5.6	9.2
25–29	40,515	47.595	2.0	1.9
30–34	n.a.	26,534	n.a.	1.1

Source: U.S. Bureau of the Census, *U.S. Census of Population: 1960.* Vol. 1, Part 1, Table 168.

over 26,000 or over 1 per cent, of those thirty to thirty-four years of age.

By 1970 probably about 15 per cent of the rural nonfarm college-age population will be attending college.

Trends in rural farm population. The figures in Table 11 do not provide a true picture of college enrollment of the rural farm population, because the U.S. Census Bureau in 1960 and in 1950 considered college students residents of the communities in which they were residing while attending college. Only a small proportion of farm communities have colleges or are within commuting distance of one. To enroll in college, a farm youth normally has to establish residence elsewhere—usually in an urban setting.

TABLE 11

RURAL FARM POPULATION EIGHTEEN TO THIRTY-FOUR YEARS OF AGE ENROLLED IN COLLEGE: 1950 AND 1960

Age	NUMBER		PER CENT	
	1950	1960	1950	1960
18	4,560	9,412	2.4	4.5
19	5,765	10,190	3.3	6.6
20	4,160	6,716	2.7	5.0
21	3,605	4,570	1.9	3.7
22	3,195	2,801	1.6	2.4
23	2,495	1,711	1.3	1.6
24	2,325	1,386	1.1	1.3
18–24	7,340	36,786	0.7	3.9
25–29	7,340	5,025	1.1	0.9
30–34	n.a.	3,393	n.a.	0.5

Source: U.S. Bureau of the Census, *U.S. Census of Population: 1960.* Vol. 1, Part 1, Table 168.

A larger proportion of rural farm youths of all ages were enrolled in college in 1960 than in 1950. The percentage increased from 0.7 in 1950 to 3.9 in 1960 for the college-age population. The proportion doubled for those nineteen years of age—from 3.3 per cent to 6.6 per cent. The increases were less for those at ages eighteen to twenty-two.

Trends of Degree-Credit Enrollments, by Type of Institution

Total degree-credit enrollment in the nation's institutions of higher education reached a new peak of 4,987,867 students (resident and extension, full-time and part-time) in the early part of the

1964 fall term. This may be compared with 3.6 million in 1960, 2.7 million in 1955, and 2.3 million in 1950, as indicated in Table 12. The increase from 1963 to 1964 was 10.1 per cent—a higher rate than in any of the seven preceding years. The enrollment increased from a low of 2.1 million in 1951 to 5.0 million in 1964, more than a doubling during the thirteen-year period.

Degree-credit enrollments in private colleges are increasing rapidly. They increased from a low point of 1,034,584 in 1952 to 1,782,084 in 1964, a 72 per cent increase (see Table 12). However, enrollments in colleges under public control are increasing still more rapidly—from a low of 1,051,990 in 1951 to 3,205,783 in 1964 (an increase of 205 per cent). Thus the task of providing higher education rests increasingly upon public supported colleges and universities.

Only in 1949 and 1951 were more—very few more—students enrolled in private than in publicly controlled colleges. In 1950, 50.3 per cent of college students were enrolled in public institutions. This figure had jumped to 64.3 per cent by 1964. Should this

TABLE 12

TOTAL DEGREE-CREDIT ENROLLMENT, BY PUBLIC AND PRIVATE INSTITUTIONS OF HIGHER EDUCATION: UNITED STATES AND OUTLYING PARTS, FALL 1949 THROUGH FALL 1964

Year	Total	Public	Private	PER CENT Public	Private
1949	2,456,841	1,218,580	1,238,261	49.6	50.4
1950	2,296,592	1,154,456	1,142,136	50.3	49.7
1951	2,116,440	1,051,990	1,064,450	49.7	50.3
1952	2,148,284	1,113,700	1,034,584	51.8	48.2
1953	2,250,701	1,203,558	1,047,143	53.5	46.5
1954	2,468,596	1,372,937	1,095,659	55.6	44.4
1955	2,678,623	1,498,570	1,180,113	55.9	44.1
1956	2,946,985	1,681,671	1,265,314	57.1	42.9
1957	3,068,417	1,780,280	1,288,137	58.0	42.0
1958	3,258,556	1,912,232	1,346,324	58.7	41.3
1959	3,402,297	2,002,868	1,399,429	58.9	41.1
1960	3,610,007	2,135,690	1,474,317	59.2	40.8
1961	3,891,230	2,352,000	1,540,000	60.4	39.6
1962	4,206,672	2,596,904	1,609,768	61.7	38.3
1963	4,528,516	2,872,823	1,655,693	63.4	36.6
1964	4,987,867	3,205,783	1,782,084	64.3	35.7

Source: U.S. Department of Health, Education, and Welfare, *Digest of Educational Statistics, 1963,* Bulletin 1963, No. 10, Table 44. The figures for 1962 to 1964 are from *Opening (Fall) Enrollment in Higher Education, 1964,* Circular No. 762, Table 2.

trend continue to 1970, as seems probable, 70 per cent of the degree-credit enrollment will be in public institutions of higher education at that time.

An important component of the enrollment increase in publicly controlled institutions was the growth of junior (or community) colleges. Between 1950 and 1960, the degree-credit enrollment of junior colleges more than doubled (134 per cent) while similar enrollment in publicly controlled institutions increased 76 per cent.

Enrollment in private and public colleges in 1960. In 1960, the U.S. Census Bureau reported that 3 million persons eighteen to thirty-four years of age were enrolled in college. Of this number, 1.1 million (39.3 per cent) were enrolled in private colleges and 1.8 million (60.7 per cent) were enrolled in public colleges (see Table 13).

TABLE 13

ENROLLMENT, BY AGE, IN PRIVATE AND PUBLIC COLLEGES: 1960

Age	COLLEGE ENROLLMENT			PER CENT	
	Total	Private	Public	Private	Public
18	469,172	197,115	272,057	42.0	58.0
19	512,089	214,084	298,005	41.8	58.2
20	410,331	174,325	236,006	42.5	57.5
21	333,256	140,297	192,959	42.1	57.9
22	211,977	85,393	126,584	40.3	59.7
23	149,513	59,044	90,469	39.5	60.5
24	128,176	51,173	77,003	39.9	60.1
18–24	2,214,514	921,431	1,293,083	41.6	58.4
25–29	444,786	175,220	269,566	39.4	60.6
30–34	345,697	85,241	260,456	24.7	75.3
18–34	3,004,997	1,181,892	1,823,105	39.3	60.7

Source: U.S. Bureau of the Census, *U.S. Census of Population: 1960.* Vol. 1, Part 1, Table 169.

At different ages, enrollment in public colleges ranges from 57.5 to 75.3 per cent. Enrollment in private colleges is highest at the younger ages. Enrollment at private colleges tends to weaken at age twenty-two and thereafter. In the eighteen-to-twenty-two age group, 41.6 per cent are enrolled in private colleges; this drops to 39.4 per cent for those in the twenty-five-to-twenty-nine age group, and to 24.7 per cent for those in the thirty-to-thirty-four.

Table 14 indicates that of the college-age population, 5.9 per cent are enrolled in private colleges and 8.3 per cent are enrolled in public colleges. The percentages are highest for both types of institutions at ages eighteen, nineteen, twenty, twenty-one. The percentages drop gradually after age nineteen. At age nineteen, 9.4 per cent are enrolled in private colleges and at age twenty-four only 2.4 per cent are enrolled. Of course, the percentages are still lower for older age groups.

At all ages the proportion enrolled in public colleges is higher than that enrolled in private colleges. At age nineteen, 13.1 per cent are enrolled in public colleges. This percentage drops for each successive age; it reaches 3.6 per cent at age twenty-four and goes still lower for the older age groups.

TABLE 14

POPULATION EIGHTEEN TO THIRTY-FOUR YEARS OF AGE ENROLLED
IN PRIVATE AND PUBLIC COLLEGES: 1960

| | | NUMBER | | PER CENT | |
Age	Total Males & Females	Private	Public	Private	Public
18	2,498,600	197,115	272,057	7.9	10.9
19	2,275,937	214,084	298,005	9.4	13.1
20	2,190,081	174,325	236,006	8.0	10.8
21	2,203,165	140,297	192,959	6.4	8.8
22	2,158,805	85,393	126,584	4.0	5.9
23	2,106,815	59,044	90,469	2.8	4.3
24	2,144,299	51,173	77,003	2.4	3.6
18–24	15,577,702	921,431	1,293,083	5.9	8.3
25–29	10,870,386	175,220	269,566	1.6	2.5
30–34	11,951,709	85,241	260,456	0.7	2.2
18–34	38,399,797	1,181,892	1,823,105	3.1	4.7

Source: U.S. Bureau of the Census, *U.S. Census of Population: 1960*. Vol. 1, Part 1, Table 169.

Projections of College-Age Population

The college-age population is certain to skyrocket. There will be at least 8 million more college-age people in the United States in 1970 than in 1960. Table 15 indicates that there will be about 1.1 million more eighteen-year-olds, 1.2 million more nineteen-year-olds, and still larger increases of those twenty, twenty-one, twenty-two, and twenty-three years of age.

The 3,649,334 who will be eighteen years of age in 1970 were eight years of age in 1960. This figure is subject to some reduction because of deaths and some expansion because of immigration during the decade. The other age groups will be similarly affected.

Nevertheless, it is certain that there will be half again as many more college-age persons at the end of this decade. The proportionate increases will be largest among those twenty-two and twenty-three years of age, followed by those twenty and twenty-one years of age.

Those in the twenty-five-to-twenty-nine age group are certain to increase about 2.3 million by 1970, and those in the thirty-to-thirty-four age group to decrease about 1.1 million.

College enrollment can be expected to increase much faster than the increase in college-age population. The differential between the two factors may not be greatly different than during the 1950's, when college-age population actually decreased 2 per cent and college enrollment of this same age group increased 33 per cent.

TABLE 15

POPULATION EIGHTEEN TO THIRTY-FOUR YEARS OF AGE IN 1960
AND PROJECTIONS TO 1970

Age	1960	1970	INCREASE	
			Number	Per cent
18	2,528,953	3,649,334	1,120,381	44.3
19	2,274,453	3,482,308	1,207,855	53.1
20	2,194,207	3,481,131	1,286,924	58.7
21	2,203,165	3,472,908	1,269,743	57.6
22	2,158,805	3,573,854	1,415,049	65.5
23	2,106,815	3,506,557	1,399,742	66.4
24	2,144,299	2,739,042	594,743	27.7
18–24	15,610,697	23,905,134	8,294,437	53.1
25–29	10,869,124	13,219,243	2,350,119	21.6
30–34	11,949,186	10,807,291	−1,141,885	−9.6

Source: U.S. Bureau of the Census, *U.S. Census of Population: 1960.* Vol. 1, Part 1, Tables 46, 155.

College and University Enrollment Projections

Projections of college and university enrollment provide bases for the determination of requirements for future facilities, staffing, and financing. The demand for college education by increasing numbers and rising proportions is inevitable. The rise in the number of potential applicants for college admission for the next fifteen to twenty years will be astronomical in comparison with the past. It is assumed in the projections presented here that the agencies entrusted to provide college education for this generation will meet the demands no less reasonably and adequately than they have in the past.

One method of projecting college enrollment is to determine its relationship to college-age population over a period of years and assume a continuation of this relationship or some slight modification thereof. In 1950, there were 15.8 million college-age persons in the United States. At the same time degree-credit enrollment of all ages totaled 2.3 million. Thus, college enrollment was 14.55 per cent of college-age population. The ratio rose steadily each year of the decade, with one exception, and by 1960 it was 21.73 per cent (3.6 million of 15.6 million). A continuation of the 1950–60 ratio trend during the 1960's indicates that enrollment should be 28.9 per cent of the population by 1970. Because the college-age population will be about 24.5 million in 1970, degree-credit enrollment should be approximately 7.1 million, or about 3.6 million more than in 1960. This 1960–70 increase, if it materializes, stands in striking contrast to the increase in college enrollment during the 1950's of 1.3 million. This projection assumes that whatever causal factors determined the attendance rates in the recent past and at present will continue to operate equally for the remainder of this decade. Obviously, actual college enrollment may be somewhat lower or higher than 7.1 million in 1970. Forecasts of school enrollments beyond compulsory school age are beset with many imponderables. All such projections become increasingly vulnerable as they extend into the future.

Projections on the basis of other assumptions are necessary. It is desirable to make projections for various segments, such as undergraduate and graduate, full-time and part-time, males and females, private and public institutions, community colleges and four-year institutions, first-time enrollment, and others. However, such breakdowns are not readily available for a reasonable period of consecutive years. The addition of Alaska and Hawaii to the forty-eight states and the District of Columbia have further complicated projection problems.

The U.S. Census Bureau published school- and college-enrollment projections in June 1961 based on different assumptions regarding level of fertility. Projections were made for 1965, 1970, 1975, and 1980. However, differences in fertility would be inoperative for college enrollments until after 1975 because future college students up to that date have already been born. Its four projections of 1970 fall college enrollment for the civilian noninstitutional population under thirty-five years of age in the fifty states and the District of Columbia are 4.3 million, 4.4 million, 4.7 million, and 5.4 million.[1]

Several recent college-enrollment projections have been made by Louis H. Conger, Jr., of the U.S. Office of Education. One of his projections is based on the relation between college education and father's education and arrives at a 1970 fall enrollment of nearly 6 million.[2] His so-called trend projection foretells nearly 7 million students.

On the basis of other equally valid assumptions, fall-enrollment projections in 1970 will probably be about 45 per cent higher than the 1964 fall enrollment of nearly 5 million. The several projections of college-age population and future college enrollments provide bases for planning purposes.

Trends of Educational Attainment of the Adult Population

The U.S. Census Bureau estimates the present illiteracy to be about 2.4 per cent, with the lowest rate (0.7 per cent) being in Iowa, and the highest rate (6.3 per cent) in Louisiana. It reports that 41 per cent of the 99 million adults (twenty-five and over) have completed at least four years of high school and 7.7 per cent have completed four years or more of college. There are 7.6 million college graduates. The gradual rising level of schooling is evident among all segments of the population and in all parts of the country and is an important contributing factor in rising college enrollments.

Years of schooling completed. Years of schooling completed may be used as one of several convenient units to indicate the upward trend. A recent report presents the following figures regarding the years of schooling completed by the population fourteen years and older, by decades, since 1900:[3]

$$1900 . . . . 7.64$$
$$1910 . . . . 7.86$$
$$1920 . . . . 8.05$$

---

[1] U.S. Bureau of the Census, "Illustrative Projections to 1980 of School and College Enrollment in the United States." *Current Population Reports, Series P-25,* No. 232 (June 22, 1961).

[2] Louis H. Conger, Jr., "College and University Enrollment: Projections," in U.S. Department of Health, Education, and Welfare, Office of Education, *Economics of Higher Education,* Bulletin 1962, No. 5, Chap. 1.

[3] Theodore W. Schultz, "Rise in the Capital Stock Represented by Education in the United States, 1900–57," in *Economics of Higher Education, op. cit.,* p. 96.

1930....... 8.32
1940....... 8.85
1950....... 9.95
1960.......10.70

The average adult American in 1960 had a year more schooling than the average adult in 1950. This is true of most elements of the population. The median number of school years completed by persons twenty-five years old and over increased from 9.3 years in 1950 to 10.6 years in 1960; among the whites from 9.7 to 10.9 years; and among the nonwhites from 6.9 to 8.2 years. The medians rose among the males from 9.0 to 10.3 years, and among the females from 9.6 to 10.9 years. The median rose among urban people from 10.2 to 11.1 years and among rural people from 8.6 to 9.2 years.[4] However, the rural-urban changes are not strictly comparable: many rural residents move to urban areas in order to secure higher education for themselves or for their children. Secondly, many rural people move to urban centers upon completing their education in order to pursue business or professional pursuits.

In 1960, 41.1 per cent of the adult population (twenty-five and over) had completed at least four years of high school compared with 34.2 per cent in 1950. Utah ranked highest in this respect, with 55.8 per cent in 1960 and 49.9 per cent in 1950.

During the 1950–60 decade, the proportion of adults with four or more years of college increased from 6.2 to 7.7 per cent. The District of Columbia ranked highest with 14.3 per cent in 1960 and 13.6 per cent in 1950.

The median number of school years completed was significantly higher in all states in 1960 than in 1950. An exception prevailed in the District of Columbia where the median dropped from 12.0 to 11.7 years, owing in part to an estimated net out-migration of 158,000 and in part to extensive in-migration from states with low educational levels. Utah ranked highest with a median of 12.2 school years completed.

The U.S. Census Bureau, through its periodic surveys, indicates much recent educational progress. Its *Current Reports, Series P-20* (January 10 and March 22, 1963), indicates that the average number of school years completed by the United States population twenty-five years old and over was 11.2 in 1962 compared to 10.1 in 1952. It shows a narrowing of the differences in the average edu-

---

[4] U.S. Bureau of the Census, *U.S. Census of Population: 1960.* Vol. 1, Part 1, Table 76.

cational attainment between whites and nonwhites. At ages twenty-five to twenty-nine the average number of school years completed was 12.5 for whites and 11.2 years for nonwhites—a difference of 1.3 years. In the older age group of fifty-five to sixty-four, the median years of school completed by whites was 9.2, compared to 6.7 years by nonwhites—a difference of 2.5 years. The Bureau also reported a 34 per cent increase between 1957 and 1962 in the enrollment in college and professional schools.

The average number of school years completed by residents of the nation is 10.6 years; in its 212 metropolitan areas, 11.1 years. The average is much higher in such large college towns as Champaign-Urbana, Illinois; Lincoln, Nebraska; and Madison, Wisconsin.

The data from the decennial federal census are not strictly comparable with the Bureau's Current Population Surveys owing partly to sampling variability. For example, a comparison of data from the 1960 Census and the March 1959 Current Population Survey on median years of school completed for persons twenty-five years old and over shows that the reported educational level is lower in the former than in the latter—10.6 and 11.0 years, respectively. The difference between the two sources arises in part from the difference between age statistics in the 1960 Census and those used in the Current Population Survey for March 1959, which were estimated by updating 1950 Census figures.

Education in relation to age, sex, and color.   Naturally, the amount of schooling decreases with age. This is clearly evident in Table 16. The younger age groups have more years of schooling than the older age groups. Presently, those in the twenty-five-to-twenty-nine age group report completion of 12.3 years of school on the average, which gradually decreases with advancing age groups to 8.2 years for those seventy-five years of age and older. Similar trends prevail among both males and females. However, the range is less among the females than among the males. Presently, the median number of school years completed by both males and females aged twenty-five to twenty-nine is 12.3 years. In all other age groups, females have more years of schooling than males and the differential increases with age for five successive older age groups. Females in the fifty-to-fifty-four age group had 10.1 years of schooling compared to only 9.4 years for the males.

Among whites, females in most age groups, especially forty-five and over, had more schooling than males. Among nonwhites, females of all ages had more schooling than males.

A large differential in educational attainment exists between the white and the nonwhite population but the differential is less in the present generation than in former generations. The gradual dying out of that portion of the nonwhite population forty-five years of age and over will gradually reduce the white-nonwhite differential.

The educational level of the population as a whole tends to rise as the older, less educated generations die out and are replaced by younger, more educated people. Thus, a gradual, continued rise in the median number of school years completed for many decades is inevitable, and especially among the nonwhite population. Educated oldsters will stimulate continued schooling of tomorrow's youth. The motivation and values of the parent generation serve to demonstrate to today's youth the importance of continuing education.

TABLE 16

MEDIAN SCHOOL YEARS COMPLETED BY PERSONS TWENTY-FIVE YEARS OLD
AND OVER, BY AGE GROUP AND SEX: 1960

Age	1960 total population	Male	Female	—White— Male	Female	—Nonwhite— Male	Female
25–29	12.3	12.3	12.3	12.4	12.3	10.5	11.1
30–34	12.2	12.1	12.2	12.2	12.3	9.7	10.5
35–39	12.1	12.1	12.2	12.2	12.2	8.9	9.7
40–44	11.8	11.6	12.0	12.0	12.1	8.3	8.7
45–49	10.6	10.3	10.8	10.7	11.2	7.4	8.1
50–54	9.7	9.4	10.1	9.8	10.4	6.8	7.6
55–59	8.8	8.7	9.0	8.8	9.2	6.0	6.9
60–64	8.6	8.5	8.7	8.6	8.8	5.5	6.4
65–69	8.4	8.3	8.5	8.4	8.6	4.7	5.6
70–74	8.3	8.1	8.4	8.2	8.5	4.4	5.2
75 +	8.2	8.0	8.3	8.1	8.4	3.9	4.5

Source: U.S. Bureau of Census, U.S. Census of Population: 1960. Vol. 1, Part 1, Table 173.

CHAPTER IV

Selection and Admission Policies and Practices

WILBUR B. BROOKOVER

*Director, Social Science
Teaching Institute
Professor, Sociology and
Education*

The rapid increase in college enrollments and the comcomitant pressure on educational facilities has resulted in an increased concern with admission policies and with methods of selecting students. A projection of college and university enrollments demonstrates that the pressure on current facilities is likely to increase rather than decline. College admission practices and policies are likely to remain a subject of much concern for some years to come. An analysis of contemporary practice and the policies, explicit or implicit, associated with the practice is an essential part of any study of college students.

The Evolution of Admission Requirements

The earliest published entrance requirements for Harvard College in 1642 were stated as follows:

> When any Shollar is able to read Tully or such like classicall Latine Authour ex temporare, and make and speake true Latine verse and prose Suo (ut aiunt) Marte, and decline perfectly the paradigmes of Nounes and verbes in the Greeke tongue, then may Hee bee admitted into the Colledge, nor shall any claim admission before such qualifications.[1]

Because the curriculum was designed for the education of ministers and instruction was carried on in Latin, this entrance requirement was appropriate during the Colonial period of American history. College instruction throughout that period was designed to prepare students for entrance to a limited number of professions. Previous formal education was not a prerequisite, but the ability to handle the classical curriculum was essential.

---

[1] John S. Brubaker and Willis Rudy, *Higher Education in Transition,* as quoted in Michigan Association for Higher Education, "Enrollment Problems: A Point of View," *Highlights,* II (1961), 3.

41

42 SELECTION AND ADMISSION

The eighteenth and nineteenth centuries. During the eighteenth century and the first half of the nineteenth century, admission requirements, as well as the secondary education program, continued to be based upon the classics. An increasing number of academies developed to prepare students to meet the college entrance requirements. These requirements became more specific during this period, and classical subjects were taught in the academies as a foundation for college study.[2]

The rise of public secondary schools and the passage of the Morril Act, providing for the land-grant college system, marked a major change in college admission practices. Both developments reflected the American desire to provide education for a larger proportion of the population. The land-grant college system emphasized the liberal and practical education of the industrial classes as distinguished from the professional education of doctors, lawyers, and ministers. Subsequently increased periods of secondary and higher education became an integral part of the complex social system.

The latter half of the nineteenth century witnessed the development of sequential patterns of high school and college programs. College entrance requirements were increasingly based upon high school offerings. The integration of secondary and higher education into the over-all economic and social system led to the introduction of various scientific and literary curricula both in high school and in college. The classical Latin reading requirement was dropped and specific high school subjects became the primary prerequisites for college admission. Because facilities were available for all who met the entrance requirements, pre-entrance selection was not common.

The twentieth century. The rapid increase in the proportion of young people graduating from high school and a slightly delayed, but similar, increase in college enrollments since 1900 have been associated with the development of various types of institutions of higher education and many varieties of secondary school curricula. Though college entrance is generally based on secondary school programs, the variations in curriculum at both levels has resulted in extensive changes in college admission requirements. These generally include specific requirements in such academic subjects as English, science, mathematics, languages, and social studies. Many colleges, however, came to accept high school graduates with little

---

[2] Frank H. Bowles, "The Evolution of Admission Requirements," Vol. 3 in *College Admissions: The Interaction of School and College* (Princeton, N.J.: College Entrance Examination Board, 1956), pp. 24–36.

regard for specific subjects. The variations in high school programs, with respect to content and quality, produced college student bodies with heterogeneous academic training. The resulting difficulty in evaluating the high school credentials presented by applicants and the pressure of increasing numbers of applicants has led to the adoption of objective test scores and other criteria in the past few decades.

Some colleges, particularly the junior colleges, admit any high school graduate, and also allow nongraduates to register for certain curricula. Other institutions, particularly those with high prestige who receive applications from many more students than they can accommodate, set up a wide range of criteria on which to base admissions decisions. These criteria, and the manner in which they are applied, vary both within a given institution and from one institution to another.

One large state university describes its practice as follows:

> The admissions decision will be based on all available evidence—school rank, test scores, principal-counselor recommendations, leadership qualities, citizenship record, caliber of high school program, firmness of motivation, and appropriateness of proposed field of study in relation to the applicant's apparent abilities.

When considering high school averages, this university is interested only in those grades obtained in the academic or "solid" subjects. The university requires prospective students to have completed at least fifteen units of high school work in particular subject sequences. Subject requirements, however, may be waived for graduates of selected accredited high schools who are recommended by their schools as being among the more able students. This flexibility illustrates both the wide range of criteria that may be involved in admission decisions and the vagueness in the definition of exactly which students will or will not be admitted. Actual admission practices can thus be changed readily without modification of the announced criteria. Such changes frequently occur from year to year in certain institutions.

The failure of many students to be admitted to the colleges of their choice has resulted in widespread public discussion and concern about contemporary college admission practices. This concern, together with the desire of educators to maximize the efficiency of the selection procedures, has given rise to a vast range of research concerned with selection practices and the prediction of college success. In addition to the studies made by individual colleges, there are several agencies that provide testing, examination, and selection services for American colleges and universities.[3] Although these agencies have, to an extent, standardized the objective criteria used, admission policies and practice still vary a great deal.

Social Implications of
Contemporary Admission Practices

Admission practices are an integral part of the conception of American society held by the policy-makers of higher education and of their perceptions of the role of higher education in that society. Few, if any institutions, can claim a unanimity of opinion or clear policy statements reflecting a particular point of view. In order to assess existing practices and the conceptions of higher education's function in the society reflected in those practices, it is helpful to construct ideal-types of these conceptions.

The "open-door" conception.   On one end of the continuum is the conception of the "open-door" college which provides higher education for all who seek it. At the other end is found the conception of the college as a producer of an intellectual elite. The "open-door" conception is reflected in the following statement from the President's Commission on Higher Education:

> American colleges and universities must envision a much larger role for higher education in the national life. They can no longer consider themselves merely the instrument for producing an intellectual elite; they must become the means by which every citizen, youth, and adult is enabled and encouraged to carry his education, formal and informal, as far as his native capacities permit.
>
> This conception is the inevitable consequence of the democratic faith; universal education is indispensable to the full and living realization of the democratic ideal. No society can long remain free unless its members are free men, and men are not free where ignorance prevails. No more in mind than in body can this nation or any endure half slave, half free. Education that liberates and ennobles must be made equally available to all. Justice to the individual demands this; the safety and progress of the nation depend upon it. America cannot afford to let any of its potential human resources go undiscovered and underdeveloped. . . .
>
> Traditionally the colleges have sifted out as their special clientele persons possessing verbal aptitudes and a capacity for grasping abstractions. But many other aptitudes—such as social sensitivity and

---

[3] Among these are the College Entrance Examination Board, the Educational Testing Service, the National Merit Scholarship Board, Science Research Associates, and the Psychological Corporation.

versatility, artistic ability, motor skill and dexterity, and mechanical aptitude and ingenuity—also should be cultivated in a society depending, as ours does, on the minute division of labor and . . . upon the orchestration of an enormous variety of talents. . . .

Incessant search for new knowledge through research, unceasing effort to plumb the meaning of life and the enigma of man's behavior through interpretive scholarship, the cultivation of gifted minds, the provision of professional education to satisfy the occupational needs of society—these are the established tasks, and their performance must be constantly improved and strengthened. But to them now higher education must add a sufficient variety of organizational arrangements and curricular offerings to encompass the wide range of individual differences in capacity and purpose that the increasing number of students will bring to college.[4]

The "intellectual elite" position.   In response, Robert Daniels expresses the contrasting ideal-type of those who would provide higher education for an elite minority:

The purpose of higher education should properly be thought of as preparation of talented individuals to render as best they can a social service and make their maximum contribution to society.

Our educational system is professedly operated according to the principle that access to education is something people have a right to. Since it is clear that a democratic society must insist on equal rights for all citizens, it follows from the first assumption that everyone has an equal right to go to college, and that any educational selectivity is "undemocratic."

Such a proposition betrays a dubious comprehension of the nature of education, even if it renders the nation's will accurately. The idea that practically everyone can and should be educated equally is an irresponsible perversion of the very essence of education. Do the proponents of the Committee's view actually believe that none should be educated beyond the level to which all can be brought, that the lowest common denominator will determine the limits of attainment for all? Undoubtedly not, for it would require the stifling of all specialized and technical training that rests on superior ability, and lead speedily to national disaster.

The President's Committee more probably had in mind the less far-fetched notion that all students should be educated together in the same system, with the more talented continuing farther. This is the usual practice—everyone swims in the same educational channel, as far as his ability can carry him; at any age level, education is the same for all, with special preferment for none. This position is still a serious threat to educational quality, since it disregards completely the importance of sequence and preparation, not to men-

---

[4] President's Commission on Higher Education, *Higher Education for American Democracy: Establishing Goals* (Washington, D.C.: USGPO, 1947), Vol. I, pp. 101–103.

tion the varying learning capacities of different students at the same age.[5]

The goals of higher education, as exemplified in the "open-door" philosophy, are: (1) to maximize human resources by cultivating all individual aptitudes and potential through a variety of programs; (2) to facilitate the achievement of the democratic ideals of an open society with the maximum equality of opportunity and social mobility; and (3) to fulfill society's needs for an increasing proportion of highly educated personnel. These goals are achieved only through provision for the higher education of all youth willing and able to use it. Anything less will tend to penalize both the individual and the society.

In contrast, the proponents of the "intellectual-elite" position maintain that the "open-door" college will not promote a democratic society because higher education for all will interfere with the education of superior leaders. Although they accept the values of democracy, they maintain that the goals of higher education are: (1) to cultivate the talents of a limited proportion of the youth who have capacity for leadership and direction of the society; (2) to maintain the maximum academic quality of higher education by eliminating those with differential interests and capacities; and (3) to provide society with a cadre of superior individuals to fill selected positions in the society. This position is also characterized by a desire, seldom expressed, to maintain the "prestige value" of higher education. A college degree bestows little prestige if most people have one. Imprisoned in the "intellectual-elite" position, therefore, is a fourth goal: to use higher education as a means of differentiating and stratifying the society on the basis of academic achievement.

Conceptions and practices. Current college admission practices may be analyzed in relation to the goals for higher education reflected in these ideal-types. It must be recognized that these types are abstractions from reality; neither one represents actual practice in any particular institution or the exact policy of any college admissions officer. In any institution, however, the practices are clearly nearer one or the other of the ideal-types. Some highly selective institutions with many more applicants than they can accommodate operate admissions programs which reflect some policies identified with the "intellectual-elite" position. On the other hand, many pub-

---

[5] Robert V. Daniels, "Is Higher Education a Hoax," *Centennial Review,* IV (Summer 1960), 354–70.

lic junior colleges and other institutions, dedicated to the education of all who seek entrance or unable to attract sufficient numbers of students to practice selectivity, operate more nearly in harmony with the "open-door" conception. The admission practices of most institutions of higher education, however, reflect a mixture of both ideal-types.

A highly selective Ivy League university with facilities and staff to accommodate only a small proportion of the very competent applicants for admission reports that its intention is to admit a well-rounded class. This means that individuals from various groups are selected so that "the freshmen classes admitted in the last several years have been . . . composed of an amalgamation of the best boys in each of the groups that apply to the college—the students, the football players, the stamp collectors, the bookworms, and so on."[6] The school, therefore, admits a considerable range of students, from all geographic regions and from all strata of society, with a wide variety of special aptitudes and interests. Although admission at this university gives an elite identification, the "well-rounded" class is not composed of a specific type of "well-rounded" individual. The announced purpose, however, reflects some acceptance of the "open-door" philosophy.

A contrary position is illustrated by the fact that some public junior colleges designed to provide education for all now admit only a fraction of the students who apply. Many more such institutions are likely to do the same as the press of students on facilities and staff becomes more serious.

Several publicly supported colleges and universities, required by law to admit all high school graduates, achieve some selectivity by counseling, flunking-out practices, and other indirect means. Such institutions illustrate another type of mixture of the ideal-types identified. Although they admit all graduates who apply, they acquire the image of a selective institution by their postadmission practices.

The fluctuation in both policies and practices of many institutions reflects the ambivalence of higher educational personnel with regard to the goals of higher education. Many of these educators want to maximize the goals of the "open-door" position and at the same time have the prestige and presumed quality accorded a more selective policy. The vagueness and variety of criteria specified for admission provides enough latitude for admissions practices de-

---

[6] Howard Gillette, Jr., and Robert G. Kaiser, "Yale Admissions-Problems and Promise," *Yale News and Review*, I, 3 (November 1962), 6.

signed to achieve a compromise between the two sets of goals. Many
institutions change their practices annually because of the turnover
of admissions officers or because a given officer leans to one or another of the two extremes on the continuum.

The absence of rigid and clearly defined admissions policies in
American higher education distinguishes it from educational systems in other societies. College curricula have not been bound by
the inflexibility of fixed entrance requirements and, as a result, our
society has been freer than others in developing many new institutions and new programs of higher education to meet its evolving
needs. Many colleges and universities have established special honors colleges with high admission standards and a highly selective
student body. At the other end of the continuum are those who
cannot meet normal admission criteria and consequently may be
directed into a general college. Both these programs are generally
distinguished from the wide range of students in the other programs
offered by the same institution.

The California master plan for higher education illustrates the
current development of state systems within which are to be found
different types of institutions. Three major types of colleges are
identified in this system: (1) the university, (2) the state college,
and, (3) the junior college. The various branches of the university
have sole authority to confer the doctoral degree in all fields and to
provide instruction in law, medicine, dentistry, veterinary medicine,
and architecture. Each of the institutions in the university system
maintains an undergraduate program, but only about 12.5 per cent
of the public high school graduates meet the requirements for admission to these programs. The specific requirements are only
vaguely stated, but they are designed to screen out all but the desired proportion of students.

The state colleges are designed to provide instruction for undergraduates and graduate students through the master's degree. All of
them provide four-year undergraduate programs and will admit
from the top one-third of high school graduates who meet their entrance requirements. The junior colleges provide two years of post-
high school education for all who desire it. Any high school graduate is admitted to either a terminal or academic-transfer junior
college program.[7] Although defined as an integrated system of higher
education, the California plan seems likely to function as a device

[7] T. C. Haly, "California's Master Plan for Higher Education, 1960–75," *Journal
of Higher Education*, XXXII (January 1961), 9–16.

for segregating the intellectually elite and establishing a hierarchy of differentially evaluated undergraduate and graduate programs. If the differentiated admissions requirements are followed, they are almost certain to lead to a system of undergraduate colleges with differential prestige and probably highly unequal quality.

Contemporary Selection Practice

For a combination of reasons, colleges and universities in America have instituted the use of a wide range of criteria for the selection of college students. The reasons for this practice are, in part, derived from the beliefs expressed in the "intellectual-elite" philosophy and, in part, from the sheer necessity to deny admission to some proportion of those who apply at many colleges. The rationale given for particular admission practices, therefore, may vary from the contention that only a limited proportion of the applicants can profit from the college's educational program to the argument that classroom, dormitory, library, laboratory, and other facilities are limited. The desire to increase efficiency by admitting fewer students and those most likely to succeed in college is a common factor in the rationale given.

The criteria.   Some institutions are under pressure to provide education for a particular public or clientele. In these institutions, certain students—for example, residents of the state or municipality supporting the institution—may be given priority. In similar fashion, some colleges select at least a proportion of their students from among the members of particular religious, fraternal, or racial groups.

The selection criteria derived from these rationale may be classified in one of two major categories: the first identifies the college clientele, support, or control groups; the second includes criteria of qualifications presumed to be predictive of success in college and/or later life.

The first category is perhaps best illustrated by residence considerations. State and municipal colleges and universities commonly differentiate between resident and nonresident students. Out-of-state or out-of-city students are charged higher tuition and extra fees in recognition of the fact that these nonresidents do not support the institution through taxation. Such institutions may set quotas for nonresidents or use other differentiated admission criteria to maintain the proportion of nonresidents they desire. Such practices tend to segregate the residents of one state or municipality from those of another.

Many colleges and universities in the past have set racial criteria for admission. Some parochial or church-related institutions set quotas, give priority, use differential admissions criteria, or otherwise extend preferential treatment to members of particular religious groups. Some public and private institutions make special arrangements for the admission of children of their alumni. State-supported institutions may waive out-of-state tuition for sons and daughters of alumni and many private institutions give some weight to the fact that an applicant is the child of an alumnus or is recommended by an alumnus. Alumni recommendations presumably are based upon academic qualifications, but many are certainly affected by other factors.

In contrast with the residential preferences of state or municipal institutions, some colleges and universities with large numbers of applicants set regional quotas to obtain students from all parts of the country. Such policies support their claim to national importance and broaden the base of their support and clientele. Similarly, state colleges and universities resist pressure to limit enrollments to state residents. These hope to avoid provincialism by mixing out-of-state and foreign students with local residents.

The criteria in the second category, those which presume to measure qualifications for success in college, are more likely to be publicly announced. Among selective institutions various criteria concerned with previous high school education are most frequently used. All such institutions require evidence of high school graduation or an equivalent level of achievement. Many institutions also require particular combinations of high school subjects. Grade-point average and/or rank in high school graduating class are also generally included among the criteria. These criteria are frequently adjusted or corrected to account for differences in the quality of the high school. A high grade-point average or rank in class from a high school with presumably low standards may carry less weight than a similar average and rank in a high school of presumably higher quality.

Many institutions now also require objective test scores for which national norms have been established. These commonly include both academic achievement tests in major secondary school subjects and academic aptitude tests. Because of this requirement, high schools have several of the most widely used test batteries administered to all students expecting to go to college.

Criteria of character, personality, motivation, and other variables are required by some colleges as a basis for making admission decisions. Data concerning these variables may be obtained from personality inventories of various sorts, interviews with the students, or reports of high school teachers, counselors, or principals. These reports are commonly one of the most heavily weighted factors in the total decision process. Several colleges and universities have found the counselor or principal's recommendation to be the best single predictor of success in a specific institution. Most, however, find that a combination of academic criteria give somewhat better prediction of college success than any one criterion alone.

Effectiveness of the criteria. The effectiveness of the criteria in selecting the kind of student body desired depends on the qualities considered important, for it is relatively easy to identify a homogeneous or heterogeneous student body in terms of residence or some other easily identified quality. But the selection of a student body composed of particular proportions of future successful doctors, lawyers, engineers, school teachers, and scientists is a much more difficult task. Many of the criteria used are valid indices of the past or present condition, achievement, or personality of the candidate, but cannot predict his future occupation or position in society. High school grades or class rank are fairly adequate indicators of past school performance. Standardized achievement or aptitude tests also reflect high school and related experience quite adequately. Inventories and interviews may measure aspirations, motivations, or occupational interests quite validly at the time and under the circumstances obtained. However, predictions of future behavior in college or after college graduation based upon such criteria will be inaccurate unless the variables remain relatively constant.

Academic performance, unlike some relevant variables, tends to be generally stable in a sizable proportion of the students. Significant correlations between the academic or intellective criteria and college grade-point averages are commonly obtained. The correlation between a combination of high school grade-point average and scholastic aptitude test score and college grades is usually about .55. The addition of nonintellective predictors usually results in no more than a .05 increase in the correlation. Because the nonintellective criteria are closely related to the intellective ones, the outlook for better prediction of academic performance in college by the addition of such predictors is not promising.[8] Much of the individual variation in the college academic performance is not predicted by the measures of student behavior on which admission is commonly based. Furthermore, the correlation of such criteria as high school grades, aptitude test scores and nonintellective factors with post college career performance is decidedly lower.[9] Some students who would be successful in college and later life may be denied admission on the basis of such criteria, while some admitted will fail to perform at expected levels.

The validity of the criteria used to select college students largely depends upon what characteristics are being predicted. Freshmen college grades can be predicted with some success. Later academic, occupational, or other personal-social behavior are predicted with very little success. Furthermore, the more effective a college education in changing the behavior of students in the desired directions, the less likely are measures of precollege performance to predict postcollege performance. Colleges which admit only those students who display the kinds of behavior desired in their graduates minimize the need to change the behavior of their students while in college.

Other limitations of these criteria have been widely discussed. Appraisals of character and personality by admissions interviewers, alumni, or high school personnel are known to reflect the biases of the appraiser. Because the norms, values, and social behavior of many students—particularly those from lower socioeconomic groups —differ from those of the interviewers, the appraisals may be seriously affected by cultural bias.

Perhaps less evident is the bias of high school grades and aptitude and achievement test scores. Fishman maintains that high school grade-point averages and aptitude tests reflect nonintellective factors in the applicant and his environment.[10] He maintains that these measure how closely a student's personality agrees with the model of the middle-class academic world. Recent studies indicate that success in the secondary school curriculum or high scores on aptitude and achievement tests may not be highly correlated with creativity or motivation for achievement, which may significantly affect

[8] Joshua Fishman, "Social-Psychological Theory for Selecting and Guiding College Students," *American Journal of Sociology*, LXVI (March 1961), 472–84.

[9] See Martin L. Gross, *Brainwatchers* (New York: Random House, 1962), and Robert L. Thorndike, *The Concepts of Over- and Under-Achievement* (New York: Teachers College, Bureau of Publication, Columbia University, 1963).

[10] Fishman, *op. cit.*

later success.[11] To the extent that such qualities are possessed by students who do not receive good grades in high school or high academic test scores, selection criteria may be biased. Unfortunately the selection practice in the American educational system contains a self-fulfilling prophecy. Children who do not do well on academic aptitude and other tests are more likely to drop out before completing high school or to pursue a curriculum that does not prepare them for college. In either case they are almost certain to lack the qualifications for college admission. Similarly, some students who are denied admission to college on the basis of high school records or other related criteria will never be able to demonstrate whether or not they have the ability to perform adequately in college. In the absence of such evidence, selective colleges continue to justify their selection procedures by the adequate performance of the students admitted.

When an institution must decide among applicants for admission, the typical college seeks to maximize the probability of successful completion of its program. It seeks a policy that will work best on the average over many acceptance-rejection decisions. When such decisions are based on criteria that do not correlate highly with the desired behavior in college, many errors are inevitable. Numerous experimentally admitted groups as well as the modest correlation between criteria and success demonstrate that many students normally denied admission would perform as well as many who are admitted. The implications of such institutional decision-making patterns for the individual are clearly indicated by Cronbach and Gleser:

> In an individual decision, the best course of action depends on the individual's value system and varies from one individual to another. A particular goal which would be worth any risk to one individual may have little value to another. Thus one boy applying for admission to medical school might value highly even a small chance of success, and would regard a shift from medicine into teaching or pharmacy as abandoning all his aspirations; another having comparable prospects of success might be contented or even relieved to abandon a medical career. Probability of success cannot be the sole consideration in the individual decision. . . .
>
> The individual decision is often unique. The choice may occur only once in a lifetime. Even where the decision can be "remade" at a later time if the first course of action works out badly, the orig-

---

[11] Jacob Getzels and Phillip Jackson, *Creativity and Intelligence: Exploration with Gifted Students* (New York: John Wiley & Sons, Inc., 1962).

inal decision has an uncancellable influence on the welfare of the individual.[12]

The affect of institutional decisions on individual students is one reason why many educators support the "open-door" policy. In such circumstances the individual decides for himself whether or not he can and should pursue a higher education. Although some who enter will not succeed, the opportunity to try remains open. It is difficult to demonstrate that such decisions are less efficient or more wasteful of human and social resources than those made by institutions.

Admission Practices in Relation to American Values and Needs

The goals of higher education identified in both the "open-door" and "intellectual-elite" positions reflect two basic values highly accepted in American society: (1) the very high value accorded the individual human being, and (2) the democratic ideals of an open society as reflected in social mobility and equality of opportunity. The advocates of both positions are also concerned with providing appropriate numbers of educated personnel, even though they differ greatly on the proportion needed. Subject to various pressures, admissions policies and practices have been developed with little consideration of either basic values or social needs. Some clarification of this relationship is worthy of brief examination. Both the "intellectual-elite" and "open-door" policies advocate support for the value of an open society with equality of opportunity and social mobility. But the two systems may not serve this function equally well. When adequate facilities are available to provide higher education of appropriate quality for all who desire it, elite admission practices in some institutions may place little restriction on the opportunity of those rejected. If other adequate facilities for higher education are not available, the restriction of enrollments to a small proportion who qualify on apparently culturally biased criteria provides no equality of opportunity for those denied admission. If more adequate criteria are devised, and accurate prediction of success in and after college is feasible, then institutional selection may maximize equality as much as self-selection. In the absence of such criteria and of equally available opportunities in other institutions, persons

---

12 Lee J. Cronbach, and Goldine C. Gleser, *Psychological Tests and Personnel Decisions* (Urbana, Ill.: University of Illinois Press, 1957), p. 7.

denied admission to the selective (and presumably superior) institutions must accept an inferior college education or none at all. This certainly reduces the opportunity for many students to achieve certain positions in life. Assignment of college students to public institutions of varying quality, as in California, is the contemporarily accepted form of segregated education. Unless one can maintain that all such public institutions are equal and that present admissions criteria are completely valid measures of fixed and stable abilities, it is doubtful that current admission practices are any more defensible under the Constitution than racial segregation.

Cultural bias and selective criteria. Although some selective admission practices result from the inability to accommodate all who apply, the advocates of the "intellectual-elite" position argue that the function of higher education is exclusively to educate a cadre of superior individuals to fill certain selected positions in the society. There is little doubt that highly selective admissions policies would produce a limited supply of competent people. Cultural bias and other weaknesses in the selection criteria make it difficult to demonstrate that the particular students selected are the best persons to fill the jobs for which they are trained. Generally, advocates of such policies also maintain that only a limited number of people have adequate capacity to profit from higher education. The college and university must, therefore, identify and socialize these few talented individuals, for much depends on the occupants of the elite positions.

Almost inextricably associated with the desire to educate a limited number of superior individuals is the desire to maintain the prestige of a college education. Although this policy might shift the basis of social stratification slightly, it inevitably establishes the process by which a stratified society is maintained. Many advocates of this position advocate a stratification system based on intellectual or educational criteria, and some maintain that such stratification is the essence of equality in a democratic society. Able people denied admission to college because their talent developed slowly or because of the bias in the admission criteria are unlikely to accept this practice as the best means of guaranteeing equal opportunity.

The high value placed upon the individual in American society and the need for increasing proportions of highly educated people converge into a common problem. Practically all educators agree that colleges and universities ought to maximize individual abilities and human resources. The "intellectual-elite" position assumes that only a limited proportion of the population has the relatively fixed capacity to do quality work in higher education. This further assumes that human potential is primarily determined genetically. All agree with Daniels that an increase in numbers of students does not mean an increase in number of brains.[13] If, on the other hand, one recognizes the importance of the social and cultural environment in producing needed and desirable types of behavior, the possibility of educating increasing numbers of highly qualified people for the society becomes a feasible goal. Higher education then becomes the means of enhancing the total collective ability of a society rather than a device for cultivating the limited ability of a small proportion of intellectually elite. Faris comments on this possibility:

> A high level of collective ability produces not only science and machinery, but also efficient organizational behavior; this in turn allows effective complex governmental, economic, and social organizations. . . . The present argument, however, is that, in a literal sense, and to an important degree, a society generates its level of ability and, further, that the upper limit is unknown and distant and, best of all, that the processes of generation of ability are potentially subject to intentional control. . . .
>
> The central implication of the present argument is that attractive potentialities of increase in collective ability are possible if we advance our knowledge of the sociological influences which stimulate and limit aspiration and achievement, and find strategic points with which we may establish some control over them.[14]

If such a possibility for increased development of human abilities exists, the demand for an ever-increasing proportion of highly educated personnel is possible of fulfillment. The admission of large numbers to colleges and universities which provide the environment for the development of such potential would seem more likely to meet America's need for educated personnel than the education of a smaller number of academically sophisticated persons.

Selection vs. segregation. The final argument to be considered is that the maximum quality of education can be maintained only by selective admission or by segregation in different types of institutions. Many educators believe that selective admission and differentiated educational programs increase the over-all achievement and quality performance of all groups.

Very little has been done to evaluate higher education in this con-

---

[13] Daniels, *op. cit.*

[14] Robert Faris, "The Ability Dimension in Human Society," *American Sociological Review*, XXVI, 6 (December 1961), 837–42.

text. The fundamental question, however, is: Does the segregation of presumably different ability levels in different types of institutions increase the total level of achievement and the supply of highly educated persons in society? Evidence from studies at the elementary and secondary level does not support the contention that homogeneous grouping enhances achievement, except among retarded students and for limited periods. In view of this, the maximization of collective achievement is more likely to occur when all are given the opportunity to learn the desired behavior in a college environment calculated to cultivate such maximum achievement. There is little evidence that the academically elite are handicapped by association with other college students. On the other hand, the segregation of students in institutions with program designed to fit their presumed lesser abilities is calculated to guarantee that less achievement will be expected of them and less provided for them to learn. Unless the various types of colleges and programs are of equal quality, the selection practices and assignment procedures are likely to reduce the total supply of much-needed personnel even though they enhance the prestige of the elite institutions.

If the goal is to maximize both individual and collective abilities, the concept of limited human learning capacity—and, with it, college and university admission policies, and the college learning environment—must be modified. It seems unlikely that this goal can be achieved by denying admission to a large proportion of the students desiring a college education or by designing college programs to cultivate the relatively fixed capacities of a limited number of academically elite. The ever-expanding need for educated personnel will probably not be met by such programs. New educational environments designed to develop unlimited collective abilities must be devised to meet these needs.[15]

---

[15] See Wilbur Brookover and David Gottlieb, *A Sociology of Education,* 2nd ed. (New York: American Book Company, 1964), Chapter 16.

CHAPTER V

American College Students
and the Socialization Process

IRVIN J. LEHMANN
Associate Professor
Evaluation Services

The socialization process plays an extremely important role in human behavior and, in fact, in recent years increased attention has been given to the role of the peer group in the formation, the modification, and the reinforcement of attitudes and values.[1] In order to understand such things as the relationship of affective measures to a student's performance in college, his choice of major, and the factors associated with his behavioral changes, one must examine the development of attitudes and values.[2]

The Development of Attitudes and Values

The child is a product of his environment. This is especially true insofar as personality traits are concerned: no one is born good or bad, honest or dishonest. There is overwhelming evidence that personality structure is shaped largely by the type of environment the child has from earliest infancy, and by the individuals and groups with whom he identifies.

The child's first identification is with his parents. By the age of five, he has taken playmates and members of his family as models. Adults outside the home are also identifying figures. The child admires those adults who are most like his parents—for example, his teachers. After some time, the child is torn between his family and peers and is confronted with a choice: Should he associate with his

---

[1] Theodore M. Newcomb, "Student Peer-Group Influence," in Nevitt Sanford (ed.), *The American College* (New York: John Wiley & Sons, Inc., 1962); Martin Trow, "The Campus Viewed as a Culture," in Hall T. Sprague (ed.), *College Students* (Boulder, Colo.: The Western Interstate Commission for Higher Education, 1960).

[2] There is an extensive literature in this field, but since we are primarily concerned with college students, specific references on which this summary is based are not identified.

peer groups in behavior which might deviate from practices in his home or should he leave the peer group?

. *Family relationships and attitudes.* The quality of the relationship existing between the child and his immediate family has an effect upon the types of attitudes and values he will develop. For example, some investigators have found that authoritarianism was positively related to parental punitiveness and that, regardless of parental discipline, those children who had favorable parental attitudes approved of this discipline, while the converse was true for those children who had negative parental attitudes.

The degree and extent to which the child's attitudes, value, beliefs, interests, and ideals may be modified depends upon a variety of factors. Some of these are the nature of the experience, the type of contact, the personality of the individual, the group's approval of new attitudes, and the subject's perception of the outcome. Some of the agents or means of effecting change are indoctrination; imitation and habituation; communication of feeling by means of facial expressions, manner, and voice; the imposition of restrictions or force to make the individual change, at least outwardly; and communication of knowledge whereby the individual in the light of new evidence critically examines his values.

Sociocultural differences in attitudes and values. The relationship between certain dimensions of value systems and background characteristics has been attracting increased interest and study. A great deal of time and money has been devoted to studying the biographical and demographic characteristics of college students.[3] Although there is general agreement that attitudes and values have their origin in the home and the family, a lack of agreement exists as to how or why certain attitudes are adopted while others are modified or altered. It is clear that differences exist among average, low, and high social-status homes not only in terms of child-rearing practices but also in the attitudes and values fostered and practiced. It is also clear that attitudes and values have their roots in the home. Hence, one should expect to find differences in the children who come from these homes.

Although a common value structure appears to be present among

---

[3] T. R. McConnell and Paul Heist, "The Diverse College Student Population," in Sanford, *op. cit.* A somewhat similar discussion is to be found in Paul Heist and Harold Webster, "Differential Characteristics of Student Bodies—Implications for Selection and Study of Undergraduates," in T. R. McConnell (ed.), *Selection and Educational Differentiation* (Berkeley, Calif.: Center for the Study of Higher Education, 1959).

people in a given culture, variations exist within and among different cultural groups.[4] Some investigators have shown that there are significant differences in values among Protestants, Jews, and Roman Catholics,[5] as well as among members of the same denomination.[6] Others have presented evidence to demonstrate that there are value differences among parochial, public, and private high school graduates;[7] children from different economic or income levels;[8] and institutionalized versus noninstitutionalized adolescent boys.[9] These studies suggest that different cultural backgrounds might result in the acceptance of different attitudes and values. However, one must not rule out the importance of heredity and personality traits.

Lehmann and Ikenberry reported a significant relationship between level of parental education and stereotypic beliefs, dogmatism, and traditional-value orientation.[10] In addition, they found that Catholic students, as a group, were more stereotypic and dogmatic than either Protestants or Jews; that Catholic students had the highest traditional-value mean score; and that Jewish students were least traditional in their value orientation. They reported that both males and females with farm backgrounds had the highest mean traditional-value score while students from predominantly urban backgrounds had the lowest mean traditional value scores. Dressel and Mayhew[11] reported that authoritarianism tended to be asso-

---

[4] Byron S. Hollinshead, *Who Should Go to College?* (New York: Columbia University Press, 1952); Sloan Wayland and Edmund de S. Brunner, *The Educational Characteristics of the American People* (New York: Teachers College, Bureau of Publications, Columbia University, 1958); Charles Morris, *Varieties of Human Value* (Chicago: University of Chicago Press, 1958).

[5] Dorothy Spoerl, "The Values of the Postwar College Student," *Journal of Social Psychology,* XXXV (1952), 217–25; Asahel D. Woodruff, "Personal Values and Religious Backgrounds," *Journal of Social Psychology,* XXII (1945), 141–47.

[6] Irvin J. Lehmann and Stanley O. Ikenberry, *Critical Thinking, Attitudes, and Values in Higher Education: A Preliminary Report of Research* (East Lansing, Mich.: Michigan State University, 1959).

[7] Charles McArthur, "Subculture and Personality During the College Years," *Journal of Educational Sociology,* XXXIII (1960), 260–68; Richard Prince, "A Study of the Relationship Between Individual Values and Administrative Effectiveness in the School Situation," unpublished doctoral thesis presented at the University of Chicago, 1957; W. Cody Wilson, "Value Differences Between Public and Private School Graduates," *Journal of Educational Psychology,* L (1959), 213–18.

[8] John K. Coster, "Attitudes Toward School of High School Pupils from Three Income Levels," *Journal of Educational Psychology,* XLIV (1958), 61–66.

[9] Richard D. Trent, "The Expressed Values of Institutionalized Delinquent Boys," *Journal of Genetic Psychology,* XCII (1958), 133–48.

[10] Lehmann and Ikenberry, *op. cit.* Stereotypy and dogmatism are conceived here as being part of an authoritarian personality syndrome—that is, rigid, unreceptive to new ideas, compulsive.

[11] Paul L. Dressel and Lewis B. Mayhew, *General Education: Explorations in Evaluation* (Washington, D.C.: American Council on Education, 1954).

ciated with orthodox and fundamentalist sects. Rokeach[12] found that Catholics were more dogmatic than either Jews or Protestants and that they were more authoritarian than Protestants, Jews, or nonbelievers.

/Clearly, then, there are differences among the different social classes and religious groups in attitudes and values. It is impossible, however, to select any one factor to account for these differences for the causative factors are intricately interwoven and continually interacting. The theory advanced by Kluckhohn may help to explain this phenomenon:

> The dominant (American) values emphasize the *Future* as the important time, the *Individual* as the important person, and *Doing* as the important aspect of personality. The alternative system relevant to the present problem is one radiating from some point in the Eastern upper class. There, the time most valued is the *Past,* the persons who matter bear a *Lineal relation* to oneself, and *Being* is the most valued aspect of the person.[13]

The Effect of Behavioral Characteristics

Choice of major. Many students change their majors while in college. The less fortunate drop out of college after spending one or two years in a major with which they have become disillusioned or even disgusted.

In a longitudinal study undertaken at Michigan State University,[14] females majoring in nontechnical curricula (such as the social sciences, humanities, and communications arts) were less stereotypic in their beliefs and less dogmatic than the females in vocationally oriented curricula (such as home economics and medical technology). Although males majoring in physical education and agriculture were the most stereotypic, those males majoring in the physical and biological sciences were, as a group, least stereotypic in their beliefs. Although there are marked curricular differences in general academic aptitude, and although there is a slight but significant relationship between intelligence and attitudes, these differences persisted even after the groups were equated for initial ability.

---

[12] Milton Rokeach, *The Open and Closed Mind* (New York: Basic Books, Inc., 1960).

[13] Florence R. Kluckhohn, "Dominant and Substitutive Profiles of Cultural Orientations: Their Significance for the Analysis of Social Stratification," *Social Forces,* XXVIII (1950), 376–93.

[14] Lehmann and Ikenberry, *op. cit.*

There is some evidence that the most conservative students tend to migrate to vocational programs or to programs of applied arts or sciences rather than to the academic fields, but this may be accounted for in terms of the social-class background of students in these fields. Numerous studies have shown that students in certain fields of study tended toward more liberal attitudes than students in other fields.

There is considerable current interest in the study of personality characteristics among students in the different majors. The groups exhibiting the most psychological problems were in the humanities while those in the physical and biological sciences evidenced the fewest; those in the social sciences tended to be in between. Bereiter and Freedman, implying a different approach to analyze their data, reported that almost all the group variation among Vassar females was accounted by only two factors: social confidence and conventionality. They explain that their findings appear to disagree with those of others because

> . . . our results show curricular groups to differ in kind of psychological adjustment but not in adequacy. Earlier studies, which did not distinguish between these components were obligated to interpret all differences in terms of adequacy of psychological adjustment. . . .[15]

Yet we know that students undergo marked personality changes while attending college and that many students change majors while at college.[16] A variety of factors enters into a student's decision to change his major: the academic demands of a particular curriculum may be too severe; the student may lose interest in his original choice of a profession or vocation; there may be a dissonance in the values of the student with his peers (or even the faculty) in a particular curriculum and he changes to a major where his behavior is reinforced; or the nature of the original major field might be such that it is antagonistic to the student's attitudes and values. In the few studies conducted to discover the reason why students change major, it was demonstrated that transfers centered around interest changes, curricular preferences and dissatisfaction, and generally

---

[15] Carl Bereiter and Mervin B. Freedman, "Fields of Study and the People in Them," in Sanford, *op. cit.*

[16] Irvin J. Lehmann and Paul L. Dressel, *Critical Thinking, Attitudes and Values in Higher Education* (East Lansing, Mich.: Michigan State University, 1962). In this longitudinal study at Michigan State, it was found that nearly 50 per cent of the graduates receive their degree in a major different from the one they chose as freshmen.

low grades. Some evidence indicates that students (especially those with poor academic records) who changed majors had certain personality characteristics—more stereotypic, more dogmatic, more inner-directed qualities—which distinguished them both from students who did not change their majors and students who changed majors but had at least a 2.00 grade-point average (where $A = 4$). The one clear fact that emerges from all these studies is that change of major cannot be explained solely in terms of intellectual deficiencies or the academic difficulties encountered in a particular field of study.[17]

Persistence in college. Because the choice of major, the stability of initial choice, and scholastic performance are related to personality traits, these same personality traits may bear some relationship to persistence in college.

Although many studies have been conducted on college dropouts, the majority of them have been concerned with the reasons students themselves give for leaving college. The researchers have concluded that college dropouts were immature in a number of ways and needed guidance and support from their families and instructors,[18] and were less responsible and independent than those who remained in college.[19] In a different approach to the study of dropouts, Ikenberry considered a variety of biographical, demographic, affective, and cognitive characteristics and found that dropouts differed from those who remained in college in terms of both intellective and sociocultural factors.[20] The data suggest that persistence in college depends primarily upon intellectual ability. Nevertheless, certain affective factors—attitudes, values, motivation, and interest—should not be neglected.

The data bearing upon the relationship between personality characteristics and choice of major, change of major, scholastic per-

---

[17] Robert V. Brass, "An Investigation of Selected Personal Background Factors and Reasons Related to Students Who Change Schools Within Purdue University," unpublished doctoral thesis presented at Purdue University, 1956; Rowland R. Pierson, "Changes of Major by College Students," *Personnel and Guidance Journal*, XLI (1962), 458–61; Wilma N. Bradley, "An Analysis of Selected Cognitive and Noncognitive Variables Relating to a Student's Persistence in a Major Area of Study at Michigan State University," unpublished doctoral thesis presented at Michigan State University, 1962.

[18] Roger Yoshino, "College Dropouts at the End of the Freshman Year," *Journal of Educational Sociology*, XXXII (1958), 42–48.

[19] Harry A. Grace, "Personality Factors and College Attrition," *Peabody Journal of Education*, XXXV (1957), 36–40.

[20] Stanley O. Ikenberry, "A Multivariate Analysis of the Relationship of Academic Aptitude, Social Background, Attitudes, and Values of Collegiate Persistence," unpublished doctoral thesis presented at Michigan State University, 1960.

formance, and persistence in college are not clear. In fact, it would appear that some of the findings are inconclusive and contradictory. Perhaps the most significant point to emerge is that there is still a great deal to be learned about the learning process and about the behavior of human beings. Perhaps more reliable instruments and more sophisticated research designs will be of assistance in arriving at both explanations.

Changes in Attitudes and Values

Most of the early investigations on attitude and value changes were cross-sectional in scope. Although studies of this type are useful insofar as understanding human development is concerned, it should not be assumed that the test scores of a group of freshmen and a contemporary group of seniors would yield the same results and interpretations that would be found in testing the same students as freshmen and later as seniors. Another deficiency of these earlier studies was the instrumentation employed. In most cases, only one or two measures were used, a select or a typical population was studied, and seldom was the interrelationship among various personality measures explored. Since World War II, however, more sophisticated research techniques and instruments have been employed, and cross-sectional studies have been replaced or supplemented by longitudinal studies. Although most of the studies on personality changes in the last decade have employed a longitudinal approach, very few of them have studied a given population at different stages of college. Instead, they have usually compared test results gathered in the freshman year with those gathered in the senior year and interpreted the data that suggested that changes occurred over the four-year period. Lehmann and Dressel[21] showed that such conclusions are misleading inasmuch as the major changes in stereotypic beliefs, critical thinking ability, dogmatism, and value orientation take place in the first two years of college.

College as an instrument of change. Implied in the objectives of a college education is the development of skill in critical thinking and problem-solving, and the development of such attitudes and values as may be acquired by an understanding of the physical universe, of the scientific method, of social organization and the process of social control, and by a study of man himself. Colleges and uni-

---

[21] Lehmann and Dressel, *op. cit.*

versities clearly desire some behavioral change in some of their students. Hence, if institutions of higher education are successful in their endeavors, one should expect to find that students change while at college. Needless to say, some students would undergo greater change than others, and some students would not undergo any change at all. In any event, one would expect that after four years of college (be it because of certain selected experiences or because of maturation), students would become more critical in their thinking, less stereotypic in their beliefs, less dogmatic, and more stable.

Jacob[22] has made the most thorough and exhaustive review of studies on college students' attitudes and values. He claimed that 75 to 80 per cent of American college students subscribe to the following profile:

> They are gloriously contented, self-centered, and express a need for religion. The traditional moral values and the Protestant ethic of honesty, sincerity, and absolutism are highly valued. Nevertheless, students have a live-and-let-live philosophy. They are "dutifully responsive towards government" but will take little active role in politics, government, or public affairs. "Students by and large set great stock by college in general and their own college in particular" but place a premium on vocational preparation.

Jacob then went on to paint a rather gloomy and negative picture of the role of higher education on personality development:

> This study has discovered no specific curricular pattern of general education, no model syllabus for a basic social science course, no pedigree of instructor and no wizardry of instructional method which should be patented for its impact on the values of students. . . . The impetus to change does not come primarily from the formal education process.

Furthermore, he states that:

> The main over-all effect of higher education upon student values is to bring about general acceptance of a body of standards and attitudes characteristic of college-bred men and women in the American community.

Nonetheless, with few exceptions, studies of the attitudes, values, interests, and beliefs of college students from their freshman year to their senior year indicate that there are marked changes. College

---

[22] Philip E. Jacob, *Changing Values in College: An Exploratory Study of The Impact of College Teaching* (New York: Harper & Row, Publishers, 1957).

students changed in the direction of "greater liberalism and sophistication in their political, social, and religious outlooks. There was also evidence of broadening interests during the college years." There is evidence of substantial personality changes in Vassar women between the time they enter as a freshman and when they leave four years later. Seniors tended to be more mature, but less stable; they also tended to be less feminine, and less authoritarian; they were more tolerant, and displayed greater religious liberalism; they demonstrated greater acceptance of intellectual values and exhibited greater internal conflict than freshmen. These findings are present in both longitudinal and cross-sectional studies.[23]

Changes in religious values. A number of studies have been made of the changes in religious values of college students. The contradictory results from several early studies are difficult to explain, but the nature of the population studied and possibly the ethos of the sample or even the element of time (with attendant changes in society) might yield a partial explanation. More recently, Goldsen[24] made a distinction between religious belief and religious commitment. She studied college students on eleven campuses, and concluded that although religious belief was widespread, religious commitment was not. A similar trend was evident in the analysis of data at Michigan State[25]—33 per cent of the males and 40 per cent of the females felt that, as they progressed from their freshman to senior year, they developed a greater feeling of the necessity for religious faith for living in modern times. In contrast to this, 20 per cent of the males and 24 per cent of the females felt that they had, as seniors, developed a greater commitment to a set of religious beliefs. But 34 per cent of the males and 33 per cent of the females felt that in their four years at college, they had become less committed to a set of religious beliefs and about an equal proportion also felt that they had become less attached to a particular religious sect or denomination.

Interviews conducted with some of these same students revealed that many of them, in the four years at college, had come to question their religious beliefs more and had become more relativistic.

---

[23] Harold Webster, Mervin B. Freedman, and Paul Heist, "Personality Changes in College Students," in Sanford, *op. cit.* and Mervin B. Freedman, *The Impact Of College, New Dimensions in Higher Education, No. 4* (Washington, D.C.: U.S. Department of Health, Education, and Welfare, 1960).

[24] Rose K. Goldsen, *et al., What College Students Think* (Princeton, N.J.: D. Van Nostrand Co., Inc., 1960).

[25] Lehmann and Dressel, *op. cit.*

These findings were also supported by Eddy,[26] who reported "a suspension of consideration and a questioning of the traditional approaches to religious beliefs." The analysis of data also suggested that Orthodox and Conservative Jewish students, and Roman Catholic students, were more questioning of their religious beliefs than were students of other religions.

Both Arsenian and Newcomb indicate that student attitudes do change from the freshman to the senior year, but they differ in their possible explanations.[27] Whereas Arsenian found choice of major to be related to changes, Newcomb found the two to be only slightly related, with community relationship the more important factor. These findings are not inconsistent and contradictory when one considers the two studies in greater detail. Arsenian was studying religious values and Newcomb was studying political values; Arsenian was studying males and Newcomb was studying females. Both investigators, however, were in agreement that changes took place while students were at college. Other researchers have come to similar conclusions, but have found that changes vary with age, sex, and cultural background.

Changes in personality characteristics. Some interesting, if not perplexing, findings are reported by Plant.[28] In one study he compared students who attended college with those who withdrew voluntarily (the groups were initially matched on ethnocentrism and intelligence) for changes in ethnocentrism and concluded that education resulted in a decrease in ethnocentrism. In another study, he compared changes in ethnocentrism, authoritarianism, and dogmatism for students with different amounts of college education, and concluded that "all groups were said to change significantly over the four-year period irrespective of educational experience during the four-year period." In both studies he found college seniors to be less ethnocentric than they had been as freshmen. Why should college appear to have impact at one time but not at another? Is it conceivable that the nature of the population changed that much in the few years between the two studies? Or is it that college may

[26] Edward D. Eddy, Jr., *The College Influence on Student Character* (Washington, D.C.: American Council on Education, 1959).

[27] Seth Arsenian, "Changes in Evaluative Attitude," *Journal of Applied Psychology,* XXVII (1943), 338–49; and Newcomb, *op. cit.*

[28] Walter T. Plant, "Changes in Ethnocentrism Associated With a Two-Year College Experience," *Journal of Genetic Psychology,* XCII (1958), 189–97; Walter T. Plant, "Changes in Ethnocentrism Associated With a Four-Year College Education," *Journal of Educational Psychology,* XLIX (1958), 162–65.

have an effect initially but that this effect is subordinate to the effect of maturation?

Not only have trends of increasing liberalism, greater tolerance, and questioning of the absolutes in life been obtained for students, in general; they were also evident when select, homogeneous National Merit Scholarship winners were studied.[29]

In the research underway at Michigan State, the freshman class entering in the fall of 1958 was tested at the beginning and end of the freshman year and again at the end of their senior year.[30] Random samples of the original population were retested at the end of their sophomore and junior years. In addition, the research staff interviewed freshman- and sophomore-year "changers." The findings of this study indicate that there were significant changes in attitudes and values from the freshman to the senior year. In nearly all instances, there was a significant improvement in critical thinking ability, a lessening of stereotypic beliefs, a movement away from the traditional-value orientation (from inner- to outer-directed), and an increased receptivity to new ideas. This was true for both males and females on some of the measures. Although these changes occurred in each of the freshman, sophomore, junior, and senior years, the major changes took place during the first two years of college. In fact, the changes in critical thinking ability and value orientation were of greatest magnitude during the freshman year and they seem to reach a plateau in value orientation after the junior year.

When these students were seniors, they felt that they were less concerned with attending college for vocational preparation than they had been as freshmen and they felt more strongly concerned with the social and academic aspects of college life. It would appear that for these students, at least, vocational preparation was no longer the primary goal of a college education.

Students became more respectful of the views and opinions of other people as they moved from their freshman to their senior year. They were now able to listen to the arguments advanced by others before drawing conclusions or making generalizations. It would appear that they became better able to base their decisions upon logical and rational grounds instead of resorting to previously held prejudices and stereotypes.

---

[29] Webster, Freedman, and Heist, op. cit.
[30] Lehmann and Dressel, op. cit. It is recognized that some of these students have already graduated while others have yet to do so, but at least all were in attendance for four years or the equivalent.

Although a proportionately larger number of both males and females stated that they felt they had developed more interest in political matters, social issues, and world affairs, the results of the interviews did not support this. It would appear that they become more interested in some aspects of politics if—and only if—it might alter their status quo. In other words, some of the students were concerned about the Congo crisis because they feared the situation might become another Korea and they would be drafted. It would appear that most of these seniors were still self-centered and woefully ignorant of the world outside the university walls.

Although Jacob[31] concluded that college students tended to become more homogeneous in their attitudes and values from their freshman to their senior year, the findings at Michigan State[32] and at Vassar[33] did not completely support this view. In fact, in only one instance (male dogmatism) was there any evidence to suggest a greater homogeneity of values in the senior year than in the freshman year.

The results of both longitudinal and cross-sectional studies, those conducted in the 1930's and those conducted in the 1960's, have demonstrated, for the most part, that significant personality changes occurred between the freshman and senior years. There was very little evidence, however, that a college education or experiences peculiar to a college environment were responsible for these changes. Changes in personality characteristics may be a function of the person's maturity or personality, a function of the times we live in, the direct result of college experiences, or a combination of one or more such factors.[34]

Permanency of Changes in Attitudes and Values

In college. Very few studies have investigated the permanency of changes in attitudes and values that came about while students were at college, and these are mainly concerned with stability of religious attitudes. Among a group of college students retested after

---

[31] Jacob, *op. cit.*

[32] Lehmann and Dressel, *op. cit.*

[33] Harold Webster, "Changes in Attitudes During College," *Journal of Educational Psychology*, XLIX (1958), 109–17.

[34] Jacob, *op. cit.;* Lewis B. Mayhew, "And in Attitudes," in Paul L. Dressel (ed.) *Evaluation in the Basic College* (New York: Harper & Row, Publishers, 1958); Morton Wagman, "Attitude Change and Authoritarian Personality," *Journal of Psychology*, XL (1955), 3–24.

fourteen years, the greatest change was in their attitudes toward the church.[35] Their positive religious attitudes had tended to persist in college although the intra- and interinstitution variances became smaller. In another retest of attitudes, both male and female alumni declined on the Aesthetic and increased on the Religious scale of the Study of Values Test, and the men declined on the Theoretical scale. The greatest change occurred on the Religious score and it was accompanied by an increase in favorable attitudes towards the church.[36] Their attitudes were the least stable; their values were the most stable. In one of the most comprehensive studies of the stability of attitudes and values, the researcher found that although there was a slight movement toward liberalism, there was a great degree of consistency between initial and final positions.[37] Other studies similarly indicate no or little significant senior-alumni differences, and thus one scholar concludes that liberalism "does not seem to be a function of the age of individuals or of what they are taught in college. . . . [It is] a product of the times." Another concludes that "those longest out of college and those who spent the least amount of time in college are more like seniors" in their attitudes. Also bearing on the question of the relative stability of attitude change is an analysis of college students in 1923, 1933, 1943, and 1953 concerning behavior they thought wrong.[38] Except for 1953 college men, small changes occurred from the freshmen to senior year. However, when the responses of the fifty-year-olds were compared with those of 1923 college students (both groups were of comparable age), it was seen that both groups marked about the same number of items "wrong." Corresponding age comparisons yielded similar results. This suggests that what is often described as "growing conservative with age" is merely the maintenance of earlier attitudes; the change is a cultural one rather than one linked to age.

After graduation. The alumni studies carried on at Vassar appear to support the thesis that there are no marked changes in

[35] Erland N. P. Nelson, *Patterns of Religious Attitude Shift from College to Fourteen Years Later, Psychological Monographs No. 424* (Washington, D.C.: American Psychological Association, 1956).

[36] E. Lowell Kelley, "Consistency of the Adult Personality," *American Psychologist,* X (1955), 659–81.

[37] Erland N. P. Nelson, "Persistence of Attitudes of College Students Fourteen Years Later," *Psychological Monographs,* LXVIII (1954).

[38] Sidney L. Pressey and A. W. Jones, "1923–53 And 20–60 Age Changes in Moral Codes, Anxieties, and Interests, as Shown by the 'X–O' Tests," *Journal of Psychology,* XXXIX (1955), 485–502.

attitudes, values, opinions, and outlook in the early years after graduation.[39] Although there were differences in the final test scores
among the various classes, it seems likely that "the differences noted
at the time of testing reflect differences which were present at the
time of leaving college." With respect to personality development
after college, the alumni-senior comparisons for Vassar graduates
suggests that "alumnae, as compared to seniors, are more stable
emotionally and more assured socially, less anxious and depressed,
generally more confident and imperturbable."

It seems safe to conclude that on some measures there were
marked differences between seniors and the same persons three or
four years after graduation; on other scales, however, there was
little perceptible difference.

The findings of the longitudinal studies at Michigan State and
Vassar indicate that changes did occur in the attitudes, values, beliefs, and opinions of college students from their freshman to their
senior year. In both studies, however, it was readily evident that the
greatest change took place during the freshman and sophomore
years. The alumni studies indicated that there was very little difference between upperclassmen and recent graduates. This suggests
that the college years may bridge two distinct developmental stages:
one stage beginning in late adolescence and terminating about the
sophomore year of college; and the other beginning in the junior and
senior years. The terminating date of the second stage is not fixed,
although it occurs some time after graduation.

Some Factors Associated With
Behavioral Changes

There is sufficient evidence to indicate that college students undergo some change in their attitudes, values, opinions, beliefs, and
interests from their freshmen to their senior year. Agreement is not
so widespread, however, with respect to those factors which might
be responsible for initiating this change.

Academic influences. Contradictory evidence has been presented regarding the impact of college on students attitudes and
values. Although Jacob concluded that, with few exceptions, neither
courses, instructors, curricula, nor method of instruction had any
perceptible impact upon student value, others have disagreed and

---

[39] Freedman, *op. cit.*

argued that certain programs were more effective than others in affecting social values.[40]

The student peer group. The work of Newcomb, Bushnell, and Hughes, Becker, and Geer has indicated the relative importance of the student peer group in influencing attitudes and values.[41] A college is a community in miniature, with its unique traditions, beliefs, and customs. Living in this community is a heterogeneous group of students (though not as heterogeneous as the nation's population), students who have come from a variety of backgrounds and who have brought with them certain traits and customs. The faculty may be considered as being homogeneous in some respects, but it may be most heterogeneous insofar as attitudes and values are concerned. Also in this college community are groups or cliques or student subcultures, each of which may have its own standards and mores. In addition to the informal, nonacademic experiences, the student is exposed to various views and ideologies in his classes. Hence, when the new freshman arrives on campus, he may be subjected to a variety of forces which might result in a modification of his attitudes, values, beliefs, and ideals.

Informal experiences. The study at Michigan State[42] reveals that—for the first two years at least—informal, nonacademic experiences played a more pronounced role in the behavior of students than did the formal academic experiences (such as courses and instructors). In fact, if one were to attempt to select the single most important experience, it would be the association with people of different races, creeds, and colors, and the exchange of opinion with them in "bull-sessions." Although the student subculture also operated in the junior and senior years, by then the impact of courses and instructors had begun to take on added importance. An interesting observation might be made here regarding the impact of courses. Both courses and instructors in the general-education sequence or in the students' major fields appeared to have a reinforcing rather than a modifying effect. Nevertheless, these academic experiences did have an impact upon student attitudes and values.

Although there are significant sociocultural differences in atti-

[40] Roy M. Hall, "Religious Beliefs and Social Values," unpublished doctoral thesis presented at Syracuse University, 1950; and Donald R. Brown and Denise Bystryn, "College Environment, Personality, and Social Ideology of Three Ethnic Groups," *Journal of Social Psychology,* XLIV (1956), 279–88.

[41] John H. Bushnell, "Student Culture at Vassar" and Theodore M. Newcomb, "Student Peer-Group Influence," in Sanford, *op. cit.;* Hughes, Becker, and Geer, *op. cit.*

[42] Lehmann and Dressel, *op. cit.*

tudes and values, there does not appear to be any evidence that biographical and demographic factors bear a significant relationship to changes in attitudes and values. At the same time, there is also little evidence to suggest that a student's major is associated with changes in his attitudes and values. Some studies have been concerned with the relationship between student and faculty values; others with the relationship between changes and the nature of the insitution; and still others (albeit few in number) have studied differences in the ability of colleges to induce changes in attitudes and values.[43]

Several research projects show that attitudes may be modified or reinforced by films, by the communication process, and by contact with other people. All these analyses have shown that, when a person comes into contact with another person or object, his attitudes *may* change. Although these and other studies corroborated previous findings that a favorable experience would be more likely to result in attitudinal change than no contact, the type of contact was very important. For example, if the contact involved a person, he would have to be reassuring, sociable, friendly, and enjoyable so that the student would tend to like and feel friendly toward him. If the contact involved films or speakers, the effect of these experiences on the student's social attitudes would depend upon the degree of similarity between his attitudes and those being conveyed.

The numerous studies on attitude and value change of college students all appear to share the common thesis that attitudes and values are both taught and caught, but predominantly the latter. There was very little evidence available to suggest that attitudes could be modified or altered by a specific course or instructor. Very few instructors or courses were recalled by Michigan State students as having a particularly potent impact upon their behavior. Several students mentioned professors who had helped them acquire a better perspective of the value of a college education but the concensus was that no instructor or course could be singled out as being responsible for changes in the basic viewpoints a student possessed when he entered college. And yet, these students readily admitted that they had changed since their freshman year. These students also

[43] Frederick M. Jervis and Robert G. Congdon, "Student and Faculty Perceptions of Educational Values," *American Psychologist,* XIII (1958), 464–66; Marjorie Hammond, "Attitudinal Changes of Successful Students in a College of Engineering," *Journal of Consulting Psychology,* VI (1959), 69–71; McConnell and Heist, *op. cit.;* Stern, *op. cit.;* Brown and Bystryn, *op. cit.;* Jacob, *op. cit.;* Martha C. Lazure, "An Intercultural Study of Personality Development in College Women of the United States and French Canada," unpublished master's thesis presented at Bryn Mawr College, 1959; Webster, *op. cit.*

indicated that the peer group had had more of a lasting impact upon their views and beliefs than had courses and instructors. They indicated that the most significant thing they had learned or that had happened to them in college was that they were now better able to get along with all types of people. It was most difficult for students to direct their thinking to one single college experience which had been "most significant" to them. Most of the students stated that the chief significance lay in a combination of acquaintances or experiences and that it was impossible for them to isolate any one from the aggregate. The analysis of the interview protocols, however, did suggest that informal rather than academic experiences were more important. Courses and instructors did assume greater importance after the students became upperclassmen, but—as has been shown —these experiences appeared to have a reinforcing rather than a modifying effect.

Although attempts have been made to assess the impact of college on the attitudes and values of students, it should be readily evident that an accurate assessment will not be possible until a noncollege group is used as a control. Changes take place between the freshman and senior years, but would these changes not occur if the students did not attend college? Plant's[44] findings suggested that college acts only as a catalyst and that there are no experiences unique to the college which have impact upon student values, attitudes, beliefs, and interests. Even if it were possible to compare a college-bound group with a noncollege group, it would still be difficult to isolate any single characteristic from the experiences of the two groups that would explain why one group underwent a greater change than the other.

A Further Look at the Jacob Report

Jacob concluded that very few of the changes observed could be directly attributed to the impact of college. He went on to say that college socializes rather than individualizes a student. Furthermore, he concluded that students were more homogeneous after graduation than they had been when freshmen.

It is indeed difficult to understand this suggested lack of impact of college on student attitudes and values when one considers differ-

---

[44] Walter T. Plant, *Personality Changes Associated with a College Education* (San Jose, Calif.: San Jose State College, 1962). See also, Walter T. Plant, *The Psychological Impact of the Public Two-Year College on Certain Non-Intellectual Functions* (San Jose, Calif.: San Jose State College, 1963).

ences in these traits among people of various levels of education. At the same time, it is difficult—if not impossible—to draw such a conclusion when one considers that very few (if any) of the studies dealt with by Jacob involved the specific question: "Do you feel your college experiences had any impact upon your behavior?" It is one thing to infer or "tease out" generalizations but another thing to analyze responses to specific questions. In addition, very little of the research reviewed employed a noncollege control group; hence, any implications concerning the impact of college on student attitudes and values are no more than speculative.

Many of the studies reviewed by Jacob were atypical in the sense that the investigator usually employed a single measure and/or only studied changes occurring during a one-year period. In addition, as Riesman[45] commented, findings for females were often discussed as if they were applicable to males and vice versa. In view of the marked sex differences in attitudes and values, Jacob's pooling of the data makes the results misleading.

Sufficient empirical evidence is available to indicate that the attitudes and values of college graduates differ from those of non-college graduates. Even if one were to assume a differential rate in the maturation process between the two groups, after a prescribed period of time there should be no differences between those who attended college and those who did not *if college did not have any impact*. This is not the case; therefore it would appear that college experiences whether formal or informal do have some impact upon student personality development. (

Another pitfall of the Jacob report involves the studies surveyed. This is not to imply that the research was invalid, but there is no denying the fact that it did vary in quality. For example, some of the studies employed standardized tests while others used original questionnaires; some employed pencil-and-paper tests while others used elaborate clinical techniques; some studied females while others studied males; some were conducted in the early 1920's and others were conducted in the 1950's. And yet, Jacob attempted to assimilate all these studies and to draw implications from the whole.

As far back as 1937, Murphy,[46] reporting on studies in the area

---

[45] David Riesman, "The Jacob Report," *American Sociological Review*, XXIII (1958), 732–38. After surveying the report in a rather thorough and methodical manner, it would appear that Riesman concludes that the evidence presented is neither pro nor con but the contest ended in a "draw."

[46] Gardner Murphy, Lois B. Murphy, and Theodore M. Newcomb, *Experimental Social Psychology* (New York: Harper & Row, Publishers, 1937).

of attitudes and values, concluded that many of the experiences related to attitude change were educational in nature. Newcomb[47] also attributed changes in the political and economic attitudes of Bennington females to the collegiate experience. In the longitudinal study recently completed at Michigan State, the impact of courses and instructors was minimal until the junior year, while nonacademic experiences and the peer group wielded greater influence on student attitudes and values. This changed when the students became upperclassmen and were engrossed in their major. There are many reasons for this change: (1) the student is blasé and indifferent in his attitudes toward courses which he feels are not directly related to his future profession or vocation; (2) the student is unable to single out any one course or instructor from the aggregate; (3) students take a variety of courses and hence topics of discussion seldom revolve about academic issues; (4) the student is not aware of the academic impact—that is, a latent effect is operating here. Because the impact of the academic experience does not appear to emerge until the student's junior year (and really becomes important only after the student becomes a senior), and because many of Jacob's studies only spanned one year, this might help to explain why he surmised that college has little impact on student values.

A large proportion of the students at Michigan State indicated that they had become more tolerant of other people, races, and religions. Many students were also of the opinion that the informal discussions in which they engaged assisted them immeasurably in developing this increased tolerance and understanding of people. As one student commented: "I now know how some people tick." These college students might have had the opportunity to engage in such discussions even had they not attended college—but would the composition of the group have been the same? Would the topics discussed have been the same? Would there have been the same degree of interaction and exchange of ideas? Although no empirical evidence can be presented, one might surmise that they would not have been similar. No doubt the topics discussed in the dormitory discussions were seldom generated spontaneously by the students themselves. On the other hand, these topics did not emerge from a vacuum. It is conceivable that an instructor or a course laid the first brick in the foundation and that the students then began to erect a structure upon it. Hence, anything which can be done to bridge the

---

[47] Theodore M. Newcomb, *Personality and Social Change* (New York: Dryden Press, 1943).

gap between classroom and informal discussion groups would no doubt be of immeasurable value in helping to bring about change. The significant thing here is that courses and instructors do play an important role—even if it is to stimulate student involvement.

Many studies have indicated that students become more homogeneous in their attitudes and values during their college years. Jacob concluded that "there is more homogeneity and greater consistency of values among students at the end of their four years than when they began." The research conducted at Michigan State and Vassar does not completely support this view. In fact, in both studies it was readily evident that the standard deviations of the different college classes varied significantly, rising and falling between the freshman and senior years. These studies also demonstrated that, with few exceptions, there is greater heterogeneity among seniors than among freshmen.

In conclusion, there is much more evidence to suggest that education tends to decrease authoritarianism, ethnocentrism, and liberalism than there is to prove the contrary. This, however, is not tantamount to concluding that education invariably decreases prejudice or liberalism. One must constantly be cognizant of the problem of definition, the factor of acquiescence, and the validity of the measures obtained. This holds true for all studies and is not intended as a criticism solely of the Jacob report. As Barton[48] stated so succinctly

> It would be more useful to keep the *means* by which values are changed (critical independent thought vs. group-adaptation) separate from the question of the *extent* of change in values. If this were done it might permit a clearer assessment of how much values have actually changed as a result of college attendance and a greater specification of the areas in which change does and does not take place.

Despite criticisms of the Jacob report, one cannot deny that it is primarily responsible for focusing attention on the role of college on the attitudes and values of college students.

---

[48] Allen H. Barton, *Studying the Effects of a College Education: A Methodological Examination of Changing Values in College* (New Haven, Conn.: Edward W. Hazen Foundation, 1959).

CHAPTER VI

College Climates and Student Subcultures

DAVID GOTTLIEB

Associate Professor
Sociology and Education

The need for the successful socialization of American youth into positions of responsibility has led to a series of studies dealing with the impact of the educational experience on student values, attitudes, and aspirations. The results of these investigations, while interesting, produce no consensus among those who have studied the college student. Although some propose that the college experience does in fact play a salient role in the development of life styles among students, others maintain that the college does little more than to solidify values already held by the student and give him a greater sense of social sophistication.

As noted in Chapter IV, Jacob's[1] conclusion that the college experience did little to alter or form student values created much concern among educational administrators, behavioral scientists and the more articulate public commentators.

In commenting on the discussion, Paul F. Lazarsfeld suggested: "The most reasonable verdict which can now be drawn on Jacob's over-all conclusions of American higher education is one of 'not proven.' "[2]

Lazarsfeld's position seems reasonable when the relevant literature is considered, for the findings are indeed inconclusive and frequently contradictory. Freedman, from his analysis of students at Vassar college, comes to conclusions similar to Jacob's.[3] On the other hand, Sanford, who also dealt with data collected from Vassar students, presents evidence which contradict Jacob and Freedman. Comparing data obtained from freshmen with those obtained from

---

[1] Philip E. Jacob, *Changing Values in College: An Exploratory Study of the Impact of College Teaching* (New York: Harper & Row, Publishers, 1957).

[2] Paul F. Lazarsfeld, In the Introduction of *College Education: A Methodological Examination of Changing Values in College* (New Haven, Conn.: Edward W. Hazen Foundation, 1959).

[3] Mervin B. Freedman, "The Passage Through College," *Journal of Social Issues,* XII, 4 (1956), 13–28.

seniors, Sanford stated: "There are also some vivid signs of growth, signs of striving for valued personal objectives, for serious purposes, for independence, for realism, for self respect, for wholeness, for intimacy."[4]

Goldsen and her colleagues tend to agree with Sanford in reporting their research dealing with students from eleven colleges. They make the following observation:

> . . . the findings of the present research call attention to what is almost a sociological truism and yet is often overlooked: that if young people are exposed to four years of institutional norms and values in the very milieu in which they are explicit and authoritative, they will become socialized to the predominant values of that milieu and will come to acknowledge their legitimacy. The present study shows that this occurs with regard to academic educational values.[5]

Given these contradictions, one might well ask: Wherein lies the fault or the problem? The fault does not always rest either with the methodology employed or with assumptions which seem to guide the researcher in his investigations of students and the socialization process. Actually there appear to be shortcomings in both areas. Apparently, many who study student behavior assume a homogeneous student population, reacting in a uniform manner to a specific college environment. The reasoning, in other words, seems to be as follows: (1) colleges do vary with regard to social and academic climates; (2) the dominant college "image" will lead to the enrollment of certain types of students; and (3) as a result of this selective process the student population will be fairly homogeneous in each institution while significant differences in student composition will be found among institutions.

The shortcomings of such an approach should be fairly apparent. First, even though institutions of higher education may be perceived differently by potential applicants, there is no reason to believe that this factor alone will be sufficient to attract students of a common background, with similar attitudes, values, and aspirations. Second, there is little reason to assume that students having the same socio-economic background will necessarily have identical reactions to all of the influences of the college environment. Third, differences in career choice among college students reflect a certain value orienta-

---

[4] Nevitt Sanford, "Knowledge of Students Through the Social Studies," *Spotlight on the College Student* (Washington, D.C.: American Council on Education, 1959), pp. 47–49.

[5] Rose K. Goldsen, *et al., What College Students Think* (Princeton, N.J.: D. Van Nostrand Co., Inc., 1960), p. 240.

tion and there is evidence to support the proposition that this factor may be as important to the general personal presentation of the individual as will be the impact of the college experience. These factors, then, are crucial to a realistic study of the impact of college on student behavior.

The methodological approach employed by those who seek empirically to understand the dynamics of the student is also open to criticism. First, stratified samples are not as reliable as longitudinal investigations. In taking students from each of the academic classes, the investigator is unable to control for student selectivity. It may well be that the students who survive the first two years of college are unlike those who have dropped out of school. As a result it cannot really be determined whether the students who remain were really alike to begin with or whether their similarities result from the college experience. A longitudinal investigation reveals what changes, if any, take place as the student proceeds through the various stages of his college career.

Second, it should be recognized that the college community contains a number of potential forces that could contribute to changes in the values of the college student. Faculty members are not the sole socializers. Peers as well as individuals outside the college setting may be contributing to the shaping of the student's attitudinal orientation. It is imperative that the investigator consider these other forces if he seeks to discover those elements in the total social system that affect student socialization.

Third, there should be more precision in the identification of *values* and *attitudes*. For example, the difficulties in interpretation which the Jacob summary has encountered seem to lie in the definition of *liberalism*. If *liberalism* be interpreted as the development of certain set ideas about the relation of capital and labor, the governors and the governed, America and the world, then the pattern of studies presented by Jacob does not seem to support the hypothesis that a college education has a liberalizing effect. On the other hand, if *liberalism* be read to mean an open-minded, flexible, tolerant, and adaptive attitude toward the world, then even Jacob must admit that nearly every study of undergraduates is a replication of the finding that college experience increases the probability of a liberal orientation. The great defect in the Jacob report, and in the work of others, is the absence of follow-up studies to show that these modifications in values and attitudes were permanent, and were not simply either adaptations to a temporary situation or manifestations of the persistence of types who were adjusted to the value climate of the given institution in the first place.

Institutional Differences and Similarities

There are three basic types of institutional factors which will no doubt play some part in the types of student subcultures which emerge in different kinds of academic settings. Each of these factors will operate to sort out the kinds of students that enter the institution and the kinds of social and academic climates that will prevail in a specific institution. These three types of institutional factors are: (1) the form of institutional control; (2) the size of the institution; and (3) the geographical location of the institution.

Institutional control. Institutional control deals with the formal organizational policies of the school with regard to administrative orientation and decision-making procedures. In some schools policy-making rests in the hands of local school personnel; in others, policy is formulated by personnel whose primary affiliation rests outside of the academic institution. An example of this broad difference can be found in a comparison of public schools and private schools. Needless to say, in both types of schools members of the academic community cannot be immune to the pressures brought by layman. In the private college or university, however, there tends to be less of a dependency or need to conform to the wishes and values of those outside the institution. In the public college, dependent as it is on state financial aid for maintenance, decisions related to school policies may be influenced or determined by those who have the power to regulate needed revenue.

This is not to say that all private schools are more or less liberal than all public institutions but, rather, that the policy-makers in private institutions often have greater control in determining who is to be educated and how. Private religious colleges, for example, can disregard the rulings of the Supreme Court and make prayer an integral part of the school curriculum. In similar fashion, the private institution can be more selective in accepting or rejecting applicants because it is not limited by state-imposed quotas. The private institution also has more freedom in deciding who is allowed to teach and what is to be taught. If a school is operating under state mandate and state law requires the teaching of a specific course, whether the faculty feels the course is worthwhile or not, the course will be taught.

It is not that one system of operational control is "better" than the other but that the nature of school control will be related to student enrollment and school climates. The public school, by the very nature of its being under state control will be more eclectic in student composition. There will, of course, be exceptions to this rule—especially in the case of public schools located in communities where racial segregation is required. Even here, however, faculty, students, and administrators—despite their own personal convictions—are virtually powerless to bring about change because the institution itself is dependent on state funds for operation.

There are other structural factors which will help to determine the caliber and nature of the student population and the school climate. The fact that an institution is parochial or secular will, of course, be reflected in the kinds of students who attend the school as well as in the type of student culture that develops. A school sponsored by a specific church or religious order will tend to have students who are fairly homogeneous in background. In addition, secular and parochial schools may also differ in the kinds of activities provided for students, as well as in regulations, and curriculum content.

Another structural factor related to student selection and socialization is whether the school is coeducational or whether it caters exclusively to males or females. Naturally the emphasis on both extracurricular activities and the types of student groups which emerge will differ significantly in coeducational schools as opposed to schools with students of a single sex.

Size of the institution. The size of the college or university is another factor related both to student selectivity and to school climate. No doubt there are students and parents who prefer the smaller or more intimate college setting where a closer interaction between student and teacher is possible. It is not unusual to hear faculty and students in large universities describe their school as a "factory"—a cold and impersonal setting in which students lose their individuality. Within the large college one is not likely to see classrooms where students and teacher are able to exchange ideas in some informal or personal manner. On the contrary, more and more large colleges are turning to closed-circuit television and large lecture sections in order to meet increasing enrollments.

The anonymity of the large school will not only determine the type of student who enters the school, it will also be related to the formation of student subcultures. Not unlike the large city, the massive university offers students numerous activities and many different kinds of people who can act as potential student socializers.

Finally, and again not unlike the urban area, the large university begins to develop its own "suburbs." As the campus population grows, additional buildings are needed for the teaching and housing of students. Gradually the institution begins to expand its borders and the campus overflows into new territory. Off-campus living increases, and as a result more and more students become physically removed from the immediate campus and tend to develop associations beyond the campus setting. In some schools students who live off school grounds enjoy greater prestige among their peers so that getting a place "on the outside" becomes a goal for many students. The greater freedom from the immediate control of school officials no doubt adds to the perceived status that comes with off-campus living and influences the types of activities engaged in by those who are not campus residents.

Geographical location. *Geographical location* refers not only to the regional location of the school, but also—and perhaps more important—to its setting. Is the school located in some relatively isolated area? Is it in some small college town? Or is it in a large urban or metropolitan area? Each of these conditions will influence student enrollment and student behavior.

Although the factor of public or private control appears to be unrelated to school size (public schools do not always have more students than private schools) and school quality (private schools are not necessarily superior), public and private schools are not equally distributed throughout the country. As Davis and his associates point out:

> . . . private unversities are concentrated in the urban East, large public universities in the less urbanized areas of the Midwest and Far West, and small private universities in the less urbanized areas of the South and Mountain states.[6]

Some students must, by force of circumstance, attend schools close to their residence—and this is the first example of the impact of geographical location on college choice. The student in the East who cannot afford to attend an expensive private school is in a less advantageous position than his counterpart in the Midwest in the selection of a college. He holds the upper hand, however, if he meets

---

[6] James A. Davis, *et al. Stipends and Spouses: The Finances of American Arts and Sciences Graduate Students.* (Chicago, Ill.: The University of Chicago Press, 1962), p. 187.

the requirements and can afford the costs of the "Ivy League" college.

Geographical location acts in still another way to influence student selectivity. Because the population of the country is not evenly distributed in terms of ethnic, socioeconomic, racial, and religious background, there will be a tendency for some student homogeneity in the colleges and universities. For example, one will find few Jewish students attending small private colleges in the South although Jews are heavily represented in the private colleges of the East. In part, this heavy concentration of Jewish students in certain geographical regions arises from the fact that there are many more Jews in the urbanized areas of the East than there are in the more rural areas of the South. In this case, the adult population distribution affects the kinds of students that will be found in different colleges and universities. The same phenomenon is in operation in the determination of the racial and social-class composition of urban state or municipal institutions. Such urban institutions are more likely than the nonurban school to enroll students from low-income and minority-group backgrounds. Naturally the lower costs of the urban school and the fact that its students can live at home will contribute greatly to the fact that the less affluent are more heavily concentrated in urban schools. At the same time, though, the urban school is more likely to attract urban students (regardless of their economic status) than students from the outlying rural areas.

The geographical location of the college operates in yet another way to attract certain kinds of students. Schools frequently reflect the local norms and values of the communities or regions in which they are located. To protect their youngsters from what they perceive as unwholesome or conflicting influences, parents may insist that their children attend local schools. The white parent in the South who tries to prevent his child from mixing with nonwhites or from coming in contact with those who reject racial segregation will probably not encourage enrollment in an urban integrated school.

Much of the same kind of reasoning appears to prompt the actions of other parents who see the college as a place for selecting a mate, for meeting "the right kind of people," and for making the proper connections for adult life.

The community environment of the college will also be related to the type of social, academic, and political climate that prevails at a specific campus. As Riesman and Jencks point out in their excellent discussion of American colleges:

It is no accident that some of the more experimental colleges have been located in the country, building an intense in-group spirit often in opposition to the hostile or indifferent "natives." Relative isolation probably helped Bennington, Black Mountain, Goddard, Antioch, and Marlboro to maintain a certain independence of current fashions in curricular organization.[7]

It would seem that in those colleges which enjoy relative isolation or which are located in large urban areas both students and faculty are spared the pressures of the nonacademic community. The colleges located in the suburbs seem to generate the greatest town-gown conflict. This tension might be explained, in part, by the fact that it is in the college town that members of the academic and nonacademic communities come into the most direct and intimate contact.

The community in which the school is located may act as a potential source for student socialization and subculture formation by its provision of activities and experiences for students. As the presence of an art museum may stimulate an interest in art, so may the presence of an active social and political movement stimulate involvement in organizations beyond the campus itself.

The cosmopolitan setting of New York, Chicago, Detroit, or Los Angeles is more likely to provide influences and activities different from those of the campus than are college towns such as East Lansing, Champaign, Chapel Hill, Mount Pleasant, or Ithaca. In the small college community, the student is restricted to interaction with people of similar background and for the most part not unlike himself. The metropolitan area, however, may place him in contact with people who represent life styles quite unlike any he has ever known.

A research report prepared by the National Opinion Research Center (NORC) at the University of Chicago indicated some of the consequences of variations[8] in institutional and structural factors. The NORC study is based on a sample of 135 schools and 34,000 college seniors representing the graduating class of 1961. Although the total NORC project was concerned with the values, goals, career plans, financial status, and academic experiences of these college seniors, the discussion here will deal only with data

---

[7] David Riesman and Christopher Jencks, "The Viability of the American College," in Nevitt Sanford (ed.), *The American College* (New York: John Wiley & Sons, Inc., 1962), p. 95.

[8] Richard McKinlay, Peter H. Rossi, and James A. Davis, *Students at the Midway* (Chicago: The National Opinion Research Center, June 1962), mimeographed.

showing differences and similarities among students at different kinds of colleges and universities.

As part of the total study of college seniors, the NORC staff sought to make comparisons between seniors at the University of Chicago and those from other kinds of academic institutions. Using an index of school quality based on mean scores achieved by entering students on the National Merit Scholarship Qualifying Test; control of the institution in terms of public or private, sectarian or nonsectarian support; and technical versus nontechnical schools, the NORC researchers established four institutional types: (1) *High-quality private* (including schools like Columbia, Haverford, and Oberlin); (2) *Ultra-Ivy* (including schools like Harvard-Radcliffe, Brown, and Williams); (3) *Midwestern non-Catholic liberal arts and sciences* (this group includes only liberal arts colleges in the Midwest, as Albion, Beloit, Evansville, Hamline, and Lake Forest); (4) *Big Ten* (including schools like Illinois, Indiana, University of Michigan, and Northwestern University). Students from these four institutional categories were then compared with the college seniors at the University of Chicago.

Background differences. The authors of the NORC report noted that the University of Chicago student was likely to have come from a different type of background than his counterpart in any of the other groups. Almost two thirds of the Chicago students came from communities with a population of 2 million or more; only 15 per cent of the students from the Midwestern liberal arts schools came from communities of that size. The majority of students from the Big Ten and Midwestern liberal arts schools came from farms or communities with populations of less than 10,000.

As might be expected, Protestants are the largest single religious group found in American colleges and universities. Yet the distribution of Protestant students varies greatly among different kinds of institutions. The largest group (87 per cent) is found in the Midwestern liberal arts schools; the smallest (39 per cent), at the University of Chicago. Catholics are most likely to be found in the Big Ten schools, with Jewish students most heavily concentrated at the University of Chicago (where they make up 30 per cent of the undergraduate student population) and the high-quality private schools (23 per cent).

Although 49 per cent of all college seniors come from families where the head of the household was either in a professional or managerial occupation, the greatest proportion of this type of student (84 per cent) is found in the ultra-Ivy schools. The smallest percentage of students with fathers in such occupations were found in the Big Ten and Midwestern liberal arts schools (49 per cent for both groups).

Although the national average showed that only 17 per cent of college students came from families where the annual family income was over $15,000, almost half the students from both the ultra-Ivy and the high-quality private schools reported such incomes for their families.

Attitudes and opinions. As would be expected, differences in background characteristics would be related to attitudes and opinions, and as a result there are variations among students at various types of schools. Analyzing political orientation, conventionality, and religiosity, the NORC investigators found the following: almost half the students in the total sample reported that they were "liberal." The largest proportion of liberals (69 per cent) were found at the University of Chicago, followed by the high-quality private and ultra-private schools (55 per cent); the Midwestern liberal arts schools and the Big Ten were least liberal (about 47 per cent).

Similar relationships are found for both conventionality and religiosity. The University of Chicago students are more likely than those from other schools to view themselves as unconventional and nonreligious. On both items the ultra-Ivy and high-quality private school students fall in the middle, with students from the Big Ten and Midwestern liberal arts schools most likely to see themselves as conventional and religious.

Occupational values. Institutional differences are also in post-college plans and occupational values. Generally, University of Chicago students are most likely to express an intention of going on to graduate school, followed by students from the ultra-Ivy and high-quality private schools, with students from the Midwestern liberal arts schools and the Big Ten least likely to indicate such a post-college intention.

As for occupational values, the NORC report indicates that students in Midwestern liberal arts schools tend to be highly altruistic in their orientation, showing less concern for "making a lot of money" and more concern with "opportunities to be helpful to others" than their counterparts in other schools. Generally, students at the University of Chicago, high-quality private and ultra-Ivy schools are less altruistic in values and more self-centered in career and occupational values.

The differences reported in the NORC study would certainly indicate that certain tpes of schools tend to attract certain kinds of students. At the same time, it should be kept in mind that the NORC data also indicate that there is variation in the background, attitudes, values, and aspirations of students in the same school. In addition, the NORC data tend to confirm an observation made in the introduction of this chapter: although the social and academic climates may differ from one institution to another, similar kinds of students can be found in most educational institutions.

Student Subcultures: Identification and Operation [9]

Generally, *subculture* may be defined as "a segment of the student body at a given institution holding a value orientation varying from that of the college community and/or from other segments of the student body."

A method of identifying these subcultures is both desirable and essential. The classificatory system adopted here is one suggested by Clark and Trow.[10] Briefly, this posits the existence of four subcultures; *the academic, the vocational, the nonconformist,* and *the collegiate.* The choice of this particular taxonomy is predicated upon the appropriateness of the terms for what are perceived to be the major goals of most college communities, and the degree to which they characterize the different student types observed. The specific subcultures are identified as follows:

Academic. This includes the students holding a value orientation closely similar to that of most college sociocultural systems. It emphasizes the "well-rounded" approach to education. Thus, although interest is centered upon a broad education, vocational proficiency and social adeptness are considered desirable and actively sought.

Vocational. This is comprised of students who accept the vocational goal with its emphasis on class attendance, study, and good grades, and who tend to withdraw from both the intellectual pursuits and the social activities offered by the institution. Being "job-

---

[9] The materials discussed here were presented initially in David Gottlieb and Benjamin Hodgkins, "College Student Subcultures: Their Structure and Characteristics in Relation to Student Attitude Change," *School Review* (Autumn 1963), 26–47.

[10] Burton Clark and Martin Trow, "Determinates of College Student Subculture," in *The Study of College Peer Groups: Problems and Prospects for Research* (Mimeographed, 1961).

oriented," they are seldom attracted to the nonapplicable aspects of academic life.

Collegiate. The students within this subculture value highly the ability to get along with and manipulate other people. Their value orientation is such that they not only enjoy social activities but also consider them indispensable to later success in life. Accordingly, they tend to minimize the intellectual and vocational aspects of academic life.

Nonconformist. The students of this subculture are, in a sense, unique, for although they come closest to the intellectual-value orientation traditionally associated with academic life, they reject its vocational or social phases together with the prescribed means for attaining their intellectual goal. They are intellectually curious, but undisciplined in their approach.

Methods of analysing subcultures. The research population used in the study of student subcultures reported here consists of all students in attendance at a large, Midwestern public university in the spring of 1962 who had originally enrolled at the university in the fall of 1958. Of the original total of approximately 1500 students, information was available on 977 students who, therefore, became the basic sample in the following analysis of data. It should be noted that although the vast majority of these students were seniors, the criteria used for inclusion in the sample was a Fall 1958 enrollment date. Therefore, a small segment of the sample were of less than senior-class standing.

Because the cognitive system of the individual is the key to adequate classification, it was necessary to devise an instrument by which the individual could classify himself into one of the four categories. To develop this instrument, a descriptive paragraph, based upon available research on student attitudes and behavior, was developed for each subculture. These statements were then read to an introductory sociology class of undergraduate students—a class more or less equally composed of freshmen, sophomores, and juniors, with a few seniors. They were asked to indicate which description was most appropriate to themselves as individuals, and why. From their answers, new descriptive statements were developed, incorporating to the fullest extent possible the expressions used by the students themselves.

These new statements were then pretested on a fraternity and a group of students judged a priori (by the authors) to fall into specific subcultures. Approximately 80 per cent of the responses on the pretest confirmed the a priori judgments. It was concluded, therefore, that the statements would be reasonably satisfactory for preliminary research.

These statements, in final form, were as follows:

Type W: This kind of person is interested in education, but *pri-*
(Vocational) *marily* to the point of preparation for his occupational future. He is not particularly interested in the social or purely intellectual phases of campus life, although he might participate in these activities on some limited basis. This person does his homework so that grades can be maintained, but otherwise restricts his reading to the light, general-entertainment variety. *For the most part, this person's primary reason for being in college is to obtain vocational or occupational training.*

Type X: This person is interested in learning about life in gen-
(Nonconformist) eral, but in a manner of his own choosing. He is very interested in the world of ideas and books, and eagerly seeks out these things. Outside the classroom, this person would attend such activities as the lecture-concert series, Provost lectures, foreign films, and so on. This person wants to go beyond the mere course requirements and will frequently do extra reading in order to obtain a more complete understanding of the world in which he lives. From a social point of view, this person tends to reject fraternities, sororities, and the social events that are a part of campus life. When this person does join, it will usually be one of the political or more academic campus organizations. *For the most part, this person would consider himself to be someone who is primarily motivated by intellectual curiosity.*

Type Y: This person is in many respects like Type X noted
(Academic) above. He is concerned with books and the pursuit of knowledge, *but* is also the kind of person who does not cut himself off from the more social phases of campus life. He is interested in getting good grades and usually tries to maintain a fairly high grade-point average. He is the kind of person who will work with student government, the campus U.N. and activities of this type. *He is the kind of person who feels that the social side of college life is not the most important but is certainly significant for his general development.*

Type Z: This is the kind of person who is very much concerned
(Collegiate) with the social phases of college life. He identifies closely with the college and tries to attend as many of campus social and athletic events as possible. This person *may* be interested in intellectual kinds of things

but will, for the most part, find greater satisfaction in
parties, dances, football games, and the like. He is concerned about his education, but feels that the development of his social skills is certainly important. His college years are centered about fraternity and sorority
activities even though he might not be a member. *This
person attempts to "make grades" but will rarely go
out of his way to do extra or nonassigned reading.*

The statements were subsequently included in an "Experience In-
ventory" containing questions relative to the student's attitudes, beliefs, and behavior. It was administered to large groups of students.

Factors associated with subcultures.   Within the framework of
the preceding discussion, a knowledge of research literature might
lead to general expectations regarding the social composition of the
subcultures, their academic performance, the amount and difference
of possible attitude change, and the differences in expectations regarding postcollege careers.

Lower-class students tend to be found in the vocational subculture predominately, with few found in the collegiate subculture. Middle-class students, although spread through all subcultures, will tend
to be found primarily in the academic. Upper-class students will
tend to be found in the academic or collegiate subcultures, with few
in the vocational.

Research on rural-urban differences indicates that rural students
should have a tendency to be vocational in their value orientation,
and not academic or collegiate. Conversely, students from urban
centers should be more academic, nonconformist, and collegiate
than their rural counterparts.

Research on religious differences leads to expectations of the academic, nonconformist, and collegiate subcultures' attraction of a
large number of Jewish students and an almost equally large number of nonfundamentalist Protestants (Episcopal, Presbyterian, Con-
gregational). Catholics and fundamentalist Protestants, however,
should be more attracted to the vocational subculture.

In terms of their academic performance, one would expect the
subcultures to rank as follows: nonconformist, academic, vocational,
and collegiate. Nonconformists are, by definition, the intellectually
curious, even if they are not systematic in their studies. Academics,
while much more organized, are committed to a "well-rounded" approach to school and therefore have less time for book learning.
Vocationals perceive school as a means to an end which may or

may not be intellectual in nature. Their commitment to scholastic achievement would be instrumental and thus not as likely to lead them beyond course requirements. Collegiates, finding their primary interest in social activities, should be hard-pressed to compete effectively academically with the other subcultures.

It would be expected that proportionately greater changes in attitudes would be found among students of the nonconformist subculture, followed by those identified as academics; vocationals and collegiates should evidence the least change. These changes, of course, are dependent upon the attitude objects considered. The attitudes considered here are those of self, religion, and authority. As an indication of the pressures of the college community toward changing the student's value orientation, a greater tendency toward an identification with the academic subculture than toward the other subcultures should manifest itself during college. Regarding religious attitudes, the secular nature of the college community should result in a significant number of students in all subcultures reporting a lessening of religious commitment. This tendency, however, should be appreciably greater in the nonconformist and academic subcultures because of their commitment to intellectual learning—nonreligious in nature. Attitudes toward authority should be uniformly less favorable for all subcultures, but the number of students in the nonconformist group changing should proportionately be greater than the number in the other subcultures.

Results. The data presented in Table 1 indicate that, on all three of the social variables considered, significant differences exist in the proportion of students who identify themselves as belonging to one of the four subcultures. As was expected, lower-class students were found to the greatest extent in the vocational subculture, although a sizable percentage are found in the academic category. Although, as expected, few are found in the collegiate subculture, they constitute proportionately about as many as those coming from the middle and upper classes. Middle-class students, as expected, were found in the largest proportion in the academic subculture. Yet, as in the case of the lower class, a sizable number of them were in the vocational category. For the upper class, as was expected, the predominate category was academic. The proportion of the upper class in the collegiate subculture, however, differed little from those of the middle and lower classes.

Consideration of Part B of Table 1 is of particular interest in that although stated expectancies were met in most cases, the anticipated

TABLE 1

A. Proportion of Students in Each Subculture Belonging to Upper-, Middle-, or Lower-Social Class (as Measured by Father's Occupation).

	Nonconformist	Academic	Vocational	Collegiate	Total	N
	%	%	%	%	%	
Upper Class	14	49	24	13	100	(244)
Middle Class	20	39	31	10	100	(507)
Lower Class	19	32	37	12	100	(78)

Total $N = 829$

$X^2 = 13.6010$ $P < .05$

B. Proportion of Students in Each Subculture Having a Farm, Village or Small Town, or Large Town or Metropolitan Origin.

	Nonconformist	Academic	Vocational	Collegiate	Total	N
	%	%	%	%	%	
Farm	22	29	44	5	100	(118)
Village or Small Town	21	40	28	11	100	(327)
Large Town or Metropolis	14	46	27	13	100	(384)

Total $N = 829$

$X^2 = 27.541$ $P < .05$

C. Proportion of Students in Each Subculture Belonging to Specific Religious Groups.

	Nonconformist	Academic	Vocational	Collegiate	Total	N
	%	%	%	%	%	
Jewish	21	45	10	24	100	(29)
Protestant I	18	45	23	14	100	(230)
Catholic	16	43	30	11	100	(146)
Protestant II*	18	38	34	10	100	(392)

Total $N = 797$

$X^2 = 20.499$ $P < .05$

* Fundamentalist and Sect

composition of the nonconformist subculture was far from accurate. Contrary to expectations, nonconformists do not come from the large metropolitan centers alone but, in many cases, from rural areas or small towns as well. It is possible that this suggests a social-alienation factor influencing rural students to a greater extent than it does urban students. This finding would further suggest that, although individuals select the same subcultural grouping, their motivating factors are not necessarily similar. Identification with the deviant group by rural youth is perhaps not so much the result of an intellectual process as it is a reaction to an unfamiliar or threatening social environment.

Expectations regarding religious differences were essentially met in the analysis of the data as presented in Part C of Table 1. The exception to those expectations, however, is found in terms of the relatively high proportions of Catholics and fundamentalist Protestants found in the nonconformist and academic subcultures. The high proportion of these groups in the vocational subcultures compared with the other religious groupings was as anticipated. Little difference is found in the proportion of religious types in the nonconformist grouping.

The data presented in Table 2 confirm the expectations concerning the academic performance of the four subcultures.

TABLE 2

MEAN GRADE-POINT AVERAGE OF STUDENT SUBCULTURES

	Nonconformist	Academic	Vocational	Collegiate	Total
N	193	384	280	106	963
X	2.72	2.66	2.49	2.32	

$$F_o(3,\infty) = 26.10 > F_t.05(3,\infty) = 2.60$$

According to the cumulative grade-point averages for the students in each subculture, the nonconformist group contains the best performers, while the collegiate group has the poorest. This finding may, of course, be influenced by variations in grading and selectivity in courses taken. Such differences are, however, significant and in the direction anticipated. It would seem that the intellectual commitment of the nonconformist, to the exclusion of social or vocational goals, allows a focus of his efforts in this direction. Thus, although the academic student "spreads himself out," in a sense, and dissipates his efforts, the nonconformist concentrates on one area. So also, the collegiate group, in its desire for social success, must sacrifice academic performance to attain its goal. Finally, the vocational group, tending to view college much as an instrument, does not have the self-commitment to intellectual achievement held by the nonconformist and academic groups: grades are important only in the context of "getting a job" after graduation.

Table 3 is concerned with the extent of change manifested by the student in the course of his attendance at college.

Part A indicates the proportion of students, by subculture, who believe that their orientation as freshmen was the same as or differs from their present orientation. The greatest shift was expected to be

TABLE 3

A. Proportion of Students in Each Subculture Indicating a Shift in Subcultural Identification Since Their Freshman Year.

	Shift to Present Subculture	Always in Present Subculture	Total	N
	%	%	%	
Nonconformist	65	35	100	(193)
Academic	70	30	100	(385)
Vocational	45	55	100	(284)
Collegiate	64	36	100	(109)

Total $N = 971$

B. Proportion of Students in Each Subculture Perception of the "Typical" Student as . . . . .

Subcultural Membership	Nonconformist %	Academic %	Vocational %	Collegiate %	Total %	N
Nonconformist	5	21	21	53	100	(189)
Academic	3	29	13	55	100	(373)
Vocational	2	20	27	50	100	(277)
Collegiate	4	13	8	75	100	(106)

Total $N = 945$

toward the academic subculture, and the data confirm this. It was also expected that the nonconformist group would evidence high change and the vocational group the least. This, too, was confirmed. What was not expected, however, was the high number of collegiate students who originally were other than collegiate. An insight can be gained, however, by considering Part B in relation to this later finding. Part B presents data on the response of students to the question: "Which of the types comes closest to describing the typical student at your college?" It is an indirect indication of how the student tends to view the general student body. Although some differences do exist among the vocational, academic, and nonconformist subcultures, the three are reasonably consistent. Approximately half or more of the members in each subculture view the typical student as a member of the collegiate group. Three fourths of the students in the collegiate subculture, however, perceive the student body as similar to themselves. Such a finding strongly suggests that this group is, perhaps, most alienated from the general value orientation of the college community. It suggests, also, that the need for emotional support may be strongest in this particular subculture.

The data in Table 4 are concerned with attitude changes relative to specific subjects, and the direction of these changes. All the data

TABLE 4

A. Proportion of Students by Subculture Indicating Shift in Their Dependence on Their Age Group for Behavior Patterns Since Freshmen.

	Less Dependent	More Dependent	No Change in Dependence	Total	N
	%	%	%	%	
Nonconformist	67	8	25	100	(192)
Academic	59	9	32	100	(383)
Vocational	53	13	34	100	(283)
Collegiate	49	13	38	100	(109)

Total $N = 967$

$X^2 = 14.346$ $P < .05$

B. Proportion of Students by Subculture Indicating Shift in Their Commitment to a Set of Religious Beliefs Since Freshmen.

	Less Committed	More Committed	No Change in Commitment	Total	N
	%	%	%	%	
Nonconformist	41	21	38	100	(192)
Academic	32	25	43	100	(383)
Vocational	30	21	49	100	(283)
Collegiate	36	14	50	100	(108)

Total $N = 966$

$X^2 = 12.642$ $P < .05$

Proportion of Students by Subculture Indicating Shift in Their Attitude Toward "The Necessity of Religious Faith."

	Less Necessary	More Necessary	No Change in Attitude	Total	N
	%	%	%	%	
Nonconformist	37	32	31	100	(192)
Academic	23	38	39	100	(383)
Vocational	25	36	40	100	(283)
Collegiate	24	32	44	100	(108)

Total $N = 966$

$X^2 = 14.771$ $P < .05$

C. Proportion of Students by Subculture Indicating Shift in Their Attitude Toward "Rules and Regulations."

	Less Respect	More Respect	No Change in Attitude	Total	N
	%	%	%	%	
Nonconformist	34	19	47	100	(192)
Academic	24	27	49	100	(383)
Vocational	19	26	55	100	(283)
Collegiate	19	25	56	100	(109)

Total $N = 967$

n.s.

appearing in this table were in response to questions phrased in this manner: "I tend to possess more (the same) (less) of this quality than I did as a freshman." Part A refers to the student's dependence on his age group for behavior patterns. Although all groups were expected to indicate a shift in this dependence, that of the nonconformist subculture was expected to be greatest; that of the collegiate subculture, the least. Part A indicates that these expectations are supported. The direction of the attitude shift is much as was expected; namely, the nonconformist subcultural group shows much less dependence on their peers than does the collegiate subculture group.

Part B of Table 4 is concerned with changes in the student's attitudes toward religion. Again, the same tendencies are to be observed; namely, the nonconformist group changes most, with the academic, the vocational, and the collegiate groups following in that order. Although directional differences are not as pronounced in B as in A of Table 4, the pattern is still evident. Students in the nonconformist subculture see less necessity for and have less commitment to a religion after college than do the students of other subcultures. It is of interest to note, however, that the academic students tend to perceive religion as more necessary and are slightly more likely to increase their commitment after four years of college. Although several explanations may be advanced to account for this variation, one plausible interpretation may be that a general commitment to the status quo results in a greater reliance on the validity of existing institutions.

Part C of Table 4 presents the data on changes in attitude toward rules and regulations. The same pattern can be noted both in the number of students changing in each subculture and in the direction of the change. Again, the academic subculture is slightly more likely to gain respect for rules and regulations than it is to lose it.

Table 5 presents data on the job expectations of the students after graduation. Although several dimensions of the employment situation can be studied, Table 5 is concerned only with their immediate plans upon graduation, their concern with income and security, and the major type of activity in their future careers. As may be observed in Part A, it is the nonconformist subculture which has the greatest orientation toward intellectual pursuits. In contrast, it is the vocational group which anticipates either career or military service as most probable upon graduation. Part B of Table 5 is of interest in that the vocational students as a group are most interested in secu-

TABLE 5

A. Proportion of Students by Subculture Indicating Their Immediate Expectations Upon Graduation.

	Career,* Job or Mil. Service	Graduate Training	Noncareer Job	Other or Don't Know	Total	N
	%	%	%	%	%	
Nonconformist	47	31	5	16	99	(185)
Academic	60	20	5	15	100	(362)
Vocational	72	13	2	12	99	(276)
Collegiate	65	12	10	13	100	(104)
					Total N = 927	

$X^2 = 43.465 \ P < .05$

* Includes Small Per Cent of Females Indicating "Housewife."

B. Proportion of Students by Subculture Indicating Type of Job Desired Upon Graduation.

	Position of Modest Income With Security	Position of Good Income— Some Security	Position of Top Income —Little Security	Total	N
	%	%	%	%	
Nonconformist	35	37	28	100	(192)
Academic	34	34	32	100	(383)
Vocational	49	27	24	100	(283)
Collegiate	24	38	38	100	(109)
				Total N = 967	

$X^2 = 28.071 \ P < .05$

C. Proportion of Students by Subculture Indicating Expectations of the Major Activity in Their Careers.

	Teaching or Service	Research	Adminis- trative	Other	Total	N
	%	%	%	%	%	
Nonconformist	53	18	16	13	100	(193)
Academic	53	10	25	12	100	(387)
Vocational	41	16	34	9	100	(283)
Collegiate	42	7	42	9	100	(109)
					Total N= 972	

$X^2 = 44.706 \ P < .05$

rity while the collegiate students as a group are more concerned with making money than are students of the other subcultures. Part C of Table 5 is of special interest in that it suggests reasons for the differences observed in Part B. For it is the collegiate group which tends most to anticipate "administration" as a major part of their future jobs. This, of course, would tend to support the thesis that the collegiate group is more interested in getting along with and manipulating individuals. Conversely, the nonconformist group, along with the academics, tends to emphasize teaching or service as a primary expectation of career activities. Generally, these findings point toward a value orientation—humanistic and intellectual for the nonconformist, and materialistic for the collegiate, with the academic and the vocational tending to fall somewhere in between.

CHAPTER VII

College Education and
Vocational Career

ARTHUR M. VENER
Associate Professor
Social Science and Sociology

The change from an agricultural economy to a mass-production industrial society has had a profound impact upon the occupational structure of the United States during the past one hundred years. The proportion of the work force directly engaged in agricultural production declined from over 40 per cent in 1870 to less than 7 per cent in 1960. Although the proportion of gainfully employed workers in manufacturing and mechanical industries remained fairly constant for half a century (about 50 per cent), the size of the group is now contracting because of increasing automation. A most significant change has occurred in the service industries: in 1910, only about 36 per cent of the work force were engaged in such industries; by 1960, as many as 56 per cent were so employed. And finally, the percentage of self-employed individuals has decreased sharply. In 1870, more than 40 per cent of the working population were independent farmers, professionals, or business entrepreneurs. By 1910, this figure had diminished to 27 per cent; today, their number has shrunk to approximately 13 per cent. In other words, a very large majority (87 per cent) of the labor force works for other people. The United States is a nation of employees.[1]

These revolutionary changes in occupational structure, economic concentration, and bureaucratic organization in both governmental and entrepreneurial activities are associated with the emergence of a new and larger middle class. Mills estimates that in 1870, only 15 per cent of the work force were engaged in middle-class occupations —management, salaried professional work, selling, and office work —whereas in 1940 a majority (56 per cent) of the labor force was so

---

[1] The data discussed above were abstracted from Leonard Reisman, *Class in American Society* (New York: The Free Press of Glencoe, Inc., 1959), p. 307, and U.S. Bureau of the Census, *U.S. Census of Population: 1960,* Final Report PC (1)–1C, Tables 89, 90, and 91.

engaged.[2] The "old" middle-class occupations—the independent entrepreneurs—have declined proportionately.

This development is to be expected in a society with an advanced industrial technology in which increasing emphasis is directed toward the service industries. In such economies more and more occupations move into the higher ranges of technical skill and specialized knowledge, for larger numbers of managers, professionals, and technicians are needed to organize, direct, and coordinate the operations of their large-scale bureaucratic institutions.[3] Because intensive and prolonged training is essential for those who would fill these important upper-level positions, society must furnish advanced education for an increasingly larger proportion of its citizens. At the beginning of this century, in the United States, roughly one youth out of every sixty was a college graduate; currently, more than one in eight is a college graduate.[4] In 1954, there were more people teaching in colleges and universities than were enrolled in 1900.[5]

Education and Occupational Achievement

There is absolutely no doubt as to the high positive correlation between educational attainment and occupational achievement—from the point of view of the status of the job and the amount of income it produces. In 1958, the average annual income for male college graduates between the ages of forty-five and fifty-four ($12,-269) was practically double that of high school graduates of a comparable age group ($6295) and nearly three times as much as elementary school graduates ($4337). It is of special interest to note that a considerable differential existed between those with some college experience and the college graduates: the former group earned over three thousand dollars less annually ($8682). Furthermore, these income differentials have increased since 1949, with the largest proportionate gains being made by the college-educated men.[6] This trend was anticipated by Glick when he estimated that

[2] C. Wright Mills, *White Collar* (New York: Oxford University Press, Inc., 1951), p. 65.

[3] See Colin Clark, *The Conditions of Economic Progress,* 3rd ed. (London: Macmillan & Co., Ltd., 1957). See also Chap. 2.

[4] Dael Wolfle, *America's Resources of Specialized Talent: A Current Appraisal and a Look Ahead* (New York: Harper & Row, Publishers, 1954), p. 6, and *Health, Education, and Welfare Trends* (Washington, D.C.: USGPO, 1960), p. 62.

[5] U.S. Bureau of the Census, *Statistical Abstract of the United States: 1957,* 78th ed., Table 51.

[6] Herman P. Miller, "Annual and Lifetime Income in Relation to Education: 1939–59," *American Economic Review* (December 1960), 962–86.

a man with a college degree may receive approximately $100,000 more in lifetime income than a man whose education ended with high school. He figured the lifetime income of those with one to three years of college as approximately $80,000 less than those who hold the degree.[7]

Not only the amount but also the source of college education is associated with income. In a study of 10,000 graduates of American colleges, Havemann and West found that median income varied considerably among the graduates of different types of institutions.[8] Their general conclusion was that the income of graduates was in direct proportion to the wealth of their colleges.[9]

The high income of the parents of these graduates was probably an important element in their attending these highly endowed institutions to begin with. Thus, the possibility exists that the parents' status was also an important instrumental factor in obtaining higher paying jobs. In short, these high-quality colleges may have been merely a passive agent in this process. But Havemann and West conclude that the quality of school does make a difference. Their data demonstrate that the students who worked their way through the better schools earned just as much as the graduates who were supported through the schools of lesser quality.[10]

The very strong positive relationship between educational attainment and level of occupational achievement is demonstrated by the fact that three fourths of our professional and technical workers have had some college education.[11] The *Fortune* study revealed that 95 per cent of the 900 top business executives under fifty had at least some college training;[12] 74 per cent had graduated from college and a significant proportion of these (36 per cent) had some graduate-level experience. The percentage of college graduates and those with postgraduate study was lower among older executives. Thus, a significant change in the formal educational level attained by top business managers has occurred in recent years in the largest cor-

[7] Paul C. Glick, "Educational Attainment and Occupational Advancement," *Transactions of the Second World Congress of Sociology*, II (London, 1954), pp. 183–93.

[8] Ernest Havemann and Patricia S. West, *They Went to College* (New York: Harcourt, Brace & World, Inc., 1952). See especially Chap. 15.

[9] *Ibid.*, pp. 178–79.

[10] *Ibid.*, pp. 181–83.

[11] U.S. Department of Labor, *Manpower: Challenge of the 1960's* (Washington, D.C.: USGPO, 1960), p. 17.

[12] Editors of Fortune, *The Executive Life* (New York: Dolphin Books, 1956), Chap. 2.

porations. Warner and Abegglen[13] have shown that in 1928 only
32 per cent of the top business executives were college graduates;
in 1952; 57 per cent were. Also, in this earlier group, as many as
27 per cent had not completed high school, while only 4 per cent
in the more recent group had not.

College and postgraduate training is becoming a prerequisite for
reaching the higher industrial positions of prestige and power. It is
apparent that the amount and quality of a person's education will
increasingly have a crucial impact on his opportunities for all levels
of occupational achievement. This, in turn, will determine whether
he will be able either to maintain or to advance his social-class
position. Colleges and universities have become the gateway through
which career-oriented youth must pass to reach the high-level jobs
which assure them of membership in at least the upper middle
classes. Viewed from this vantage point, the colleges have become the
"watchdogs" of the upper middle classes; the initiation rite which
separates them from the lower middle classes.[14] To join the "diploma elite" as Packard puts it, is to become one of those "big,
active, successful people who pretty much run things."[15]

Education and Occupational Mobility

In the days before big business and big government were dominant cultural forces, alternative pathways to success existed. The
typical steps were to accrue a sufficient amount of capital to launch
a small business endeavor which could be expanded through vigor-
ous competition with other small businessmen. The clerk became a
salesman and then a merchant; the industrial worker rose to fore-
man and later became a manufacturer; the sharecropper bought his
own parcel of land and became a profit-seeking farmer. These typical entrepreneural success patterns are founded on an economic
structure characterized by small proprietorship. Today, few individuals can accumulate the capital necessary to start a business
able to compete with the large corporate complexes. Higher educa-

[13] W. Lloyd Warner and James C. Abegglen, *Occupational Mobility in American Business and Industry, 1928–52* (Minneapolis: University of Minnesota Press,
1955), p. 108.

[14] This theme is more fully developed in David Riesman and Christopher Jencks,
"The Viability of the American College," in Nevitt Sanford (ed.), *The American
College* (New York: John Wiley & Sons, Inc., 1962), pp. 74–104.

[15] Vance Packard, *The Status Seekers* (New York: David McKay Co., Inc.,
1959), pp. 38–39.

tion has become the prime avenue for occupational mobility. In order to maintain an open-class society, this remaining pathway to better jobs must be available to a broader segment of the population.

Mulligan's review of numerous studies revealed the following relationships between socioeconomic status and access to high school and college education:[16]

1. Students from professional, proprietor, and managerial groups tend to increase in proportion from grammar school to college.
2. Students in liberal arts colleges tend to stand higher in the socio-economic scale than those in teachers colleges and normal schools.
3. Students enrolled in private schools and universities, on the whole, come from higher socioeconomic groups than students attending public high schools, junior colleges, or state universities.
4. Students from the upper socioeconomic groups are overrepresented in institutions of higher learning, and students from the lower socio-economic groups are underrepresented.
5. The chances that a child of superior intelligence has of attending college increase as his father's occupational status increases.

In a study of 1444 Indiana University men students in 1947, Mulligan found that the lack of talented students from farming, semiskilled and unskilled occupational groups resulted from both economic and cultural (motivational) factors.[17] Even though veterans were included in the study, socioeconomic status and access to college were positively correlated. The professional groups produced the largest proportion of students, 13.9 per cent, although these occupations comprised only 4.2 per cent of the Indiana population at that time. On the other hand, the semiskilled occupations produced the smallest proportion of students although they comprised 19.4 per cent of the state's population. The disadvantage of students from the less skilled occupations would have been greater without the veterans: the author estimated that the G.I. Bill increased the proportion of such students by more than 90 per cent.

Rogoff's study of over 35,000 American high school seniors, in over 500 schools revealed the influence of both family background and scholastic ability on the decision to go to college.[18] Scholastic

---

[16] Raymond A. Mulligan, "Socioeconomic Background and College Enrollment," *American Sociological Review,* XVI (1951), 188–96. Quote from p. 188. For a comprehensive review of such data, see S. M. Lipset and Reinhard Bendix, *Social Mobility in an Industrial Society* (Berkeley and Los Angeles: University of California Press, 1960). See especially Chap. 9.

[17] Mulligan, *op. cit.*

[18] Natalie Rogoff, "Local Social Structure and Educational Selection," in A. H. Halsey, Jean Floud, and C. Arnold Anderson (eds.) *Education, Economy, and Society* (New York: The Free Press of Glencoe, Inc., 1961), pp. 241–51.

ability was measured by a twenty-item test especially developed for the study by the Educational Testing Service. The index of family socioeducational status was based upon a combination of father's occupational status, father's educational attainment, and college attendance of older sisters and brothers.

Scholastic ability was clearly associated with the student's plans to go to college. Data shown in Table 1 indicate that 61 per cent of the students in the top scholastic ability quartile expressed plans to go to college, while only 24 per cent of the bottom quartile had such desires. However, it is also clear that higher educational plans are affected by the socioeducational status of their families: 72 per cent of the youth from the highest socioeducational quintile families expected to go to college, but only 24 per cent of the lowest quintile were so inclined. The data clearly demonstrate that the two factors —socioeducational status and scholastic ability—reinforce one another in their influence on the student's plans for further education. Eighty-three per cent of the most capable youth from the highest-status families planned to enter college, but only 18 per cent of the lowest-ability students from the lowest-status backgrounds had college training in mind. Further, a majority (53 per cent) of the youngsters from the highest-status families planned to go to college, but at no level of competence were a majority of the sons and daughters of the low-status families college-oriented.

The school plays a vital role in the determination of who will strive toward higher educational goals. Rogoff's data showed that the social status of the student's family and the type of high school attended were about equal in influence. Youngsters who were attending high schools in the suburbs with a population of 10,000 to 49,999 had the greatest college-going potential. Furthermore, all students, regardless of social-class background, emerged from the better suburban schools with more academic potential than those educated in small villages or large industrial cities.

Many other cultural factors limit or enhance higher educational attainment.[19] For example, in Chapter III, it was shown that Negroes are very much underrepresented in colleges. It is important to note that it is impossible to predict college attendance with complete accuracy from any one or more of these variables. Numerous un-

---

[19] For a consideration of some of the psychological elements, see Elizabeth Douvan and Carol Kaye, "Motivational Factors in College Entrance," in Sanford, op. cit., pp. 199–224.

TABLE 1

PER CENT OF HIGH SCHOOL SENIORS PLANNING TO ATTEND COLLEGE,
ACCORDING TO SCHOLASTIC ABILITY (IN QUARTILES) AND
SOCIOEDUCATIONAL STATUS OF THE FAMILY

Scholastic ability quartile		Family Status Quintile						
		(High) 5	4	3	2	(Low) 1	All quintiles	N
(High)	4	83	66	53	44	43	61	(8,647)
	3	70	53	37	29	29	44	(8,709)
	2	65	41	31	21	21	33	(8,696)
(Low)	1	53	30	22	16	18	24	(8,509)
All quartiles		72	47	35	26	24	40	
N		(6,520)	(6,647)	(6,465)	(8,116)	(6,811)		(34,561)

Source: NATALIE ROGOFF, "Local Social Structure and Educational Selection," in A. H. Halsey, Jean Floud, and C. Arnold Anderson (eds.), *Education, Economy, and Society* (New York: The Free Press of Glencoe, Inc.) 1961, p. 246.

expected factors diminish the accuracy of such predictions. For example:

> . . . the gifted child of middle-class parents who wants to be a jazz saxophonist and shows no interest in academic training, the boy of middling-high intelligence who wins high grades and election to Phi Beta Kappa, the son of Italian immigrants who finished medical school despite what seem insurmountable financial problems.[20]

Rogoff's study indicates that more than two out of five (43 per cent) high-ability children whose families were in the lowest-status quintile planned to enroll in college. Other research data show comparable proportions. What differentiates these high-ability lower-class youth who plan a college career from the majority of their peers who have no such aspirations? Recent studies indicate that, typically, the parents of these upwardly oriented youth—dissatisfied with their station in life—transfer feelings of deprivation to the child in the form of a strong mobility drive. At a very early age, such children are inculcated with the notion that education is the only pathway to success.

This upward "push" is reinforced by the kinds of friends the child tends to choose.[21] Simpson has shown that upwardly mobile work-

---

[20] *Ibid.,* p. 199. See also Wilbur Brookover and David Gottlieb, *A Sociology of Education,* 2nd ed. (New York: American Book Company, 1964), Chap. 2.

[21] See Joseph A. Kahl, "Educational and Occupational Aspirations of 'Common Man' Boys," *Harvard Educational Review,* XXIII (Summer 1953), 186–203; and Joseph A. Kahl, *The American Class Structure* (New York: Holt, Rinehart & Winston, Inc., 1957), pp. 281–89.

ing-class boys have many more middle-class friends than nonmobile working-class boys.[22] Furthermore, his data revealed that these mobile working-class boys belonged to about as many extracurricular clubs as the ambitious middle-class youngsters, considerably more than the unambitious middle-class boys, and more than twice as many as their nonmobile working-class peers.

Individuals outside the family help to direct and encourage these mobile youth. In a study of 194 matriculants at Stanford University, Ellis and Lane found that teachers were a chief source of support outside the family.[23] Based upon comments made by these students during interviews, the authors conclude that the public school does bring the student into close personal contact with teachers with whom they discuss career plans. Also, these instructors help the child maintain his motivation for high educational achievement. As many as 68 per cent of the students from the lowest social classes mentioned the teacher as a source of guidance in the selection of an undergraduate major. Teachers, however, were not the only middle-class models for the lower-class mobile youth. Other adults, such as ministers, family friends, previous employers, and family physicians are also employed by lower-class youth as middle-class role-models.

Warner and Abegglen, in delineating the typical career pattern of the top business executives from relatively humble family backgrounds, report that they were trying to flee as well as trying to achieve.[24] Something in their home environment was deeply repugnant—many viewed their fathers as failures: weak and uninformed, intemperate, and irresponsible men who were unable to support the family adequately. In addition, their mothers continuously inculcated them with the notion that they had to be better than their fathers.

This escape syndrome, including the tendency of mobile lower-class youth to rely heavily on adults outside the family for appropriate role-models, is an aspect of what Merton has referred to as the *disassociative* consequences of upward social mobility.[25] It is to be expected then that these mobile persons will have a high degree

---

[22] Richard L. Simpson, "Parental Influence, Anticipatory Socialization, and Social Mobility," *American Sociological Revew,* XXVII (August 1962), 517–22.

[23] Robert A. Ellis and W. Clayton Lane, "Structural Supports for Upward Mobility," *American Sociological Review,* XXVIII (October 1963), 743–56.

[24] Warner and Abegglen, *op. cit.*

[25] Robert K. Merton, *Social Theory and Social Structure,* rev. ed. (New York: The Free Press of Glencoe, Inc., 1957).

of ambivalence toward their parents. Data from a nationwide survey of high school boys and girls show this to be the case.[26] College male aspirants from the lower-middle-class and working-class families, when contrasted with those from the same status who did not plan on going to college were: (1) less likely to choose a family member as an "adult ideal," (2) more apt to feel that "friendship can be as intimate as a family tie," (3) more predisposed to react negatively to parental restriction, and (4) more likely to be in disagreement with their parents. Girls showed similar evidence of disassociation when asked to respond to a projective test which raised the dilemma of a girl with a good job away from home whose mother asked her to return home because she (the mother) was lonely. A greater percentage of college-oriented girls from the lower strata would refuse to return home or would offer some compromise suggestion than those girls who did not aspire to college. And the college girls also suggested more frequently than did the non-college group that overprotectiveness and restrictiveness were objectionable traits in parents.

Profile of the American College Graduate

Everyone has some impression of the type of graduate who emerges from four years of college to join the "diploma elite." A recently completed comprehensive survey by the National Opinion Research Center of approximately 35,000 graduating seniors from 135 colleges and universities provides a chance to check the accuracy of these impressions.[27] Davis presents the following composite profile of the model June 1961 graduate:[28]

> The model graduates of June 1961 were more likely to be men than women, were in their early twenties, came from families where they were neither the youngest nor the oldest, nor the only child, were unmarried, and were white, native-born Americans, from cities of over 100,000. They were members of the middle and upper middle class whose fathers and mothers had at least graduated from high school, and whose income was over $7500. Their fathers were managers or professionals. The graduates had at least a part-

---

[26] Douvan and Kaye, *op. cit.*, pp. 209–12. This evidence was suggested by Ellis and Lane, *op. cit.*, p. 756 n.

[27] James A. Davis, *Great Expectations: Volume One* (Chicago: The University of Chicago: National Opinion Research Center, 1963). Because of the richness of the data, the proceeding statistical statements will be abstracted from this report, unless otherwise noted.

[28] *Ibid.*, pp. 8–9.

time job during their final year of college, and were still members of the Protestant religion in which they had been raised.

They had warm and positive feelings toward their schools and professors, planned to continue their education in graduate school (at least eventually), planned to be some kind of professional (if one counts education from elementary to university as a profession), did not particularly like businessmen, had at least a B average, thought of themselves as being in the top one fourth of their class, and found intellectual and service values the most important things they would look for in their job. While they were in school they had lived in a dormitory or in off-campus housing and were within four hours' driving time from their family.

They thought of themselves as conventional, religious, and politically liberal, and were inclined to describe themselves as cooperative, ambitious, happy, fun-loving, easygoing, idealistic, athletic, and cautious.

The data revealed that only 3 per cent of the sample were Negroes, and these typically came from small cities, were more likely to be Protestant, demonstrated much less academic accomplishment, and included proportionately more females. Seniors from the larger cities (100,000 or more inhabitants) and suburbs had higher social-status backgrounds, had a smaller proportion of Protestants, and demonstrated higher academic performance. A greater proportion of Jews, larger-city Protestants, coeds, and high academic performers were in the higher socioeconomic-status groups.

Protestants comprised the largest religious group (60 per cent) and were disproportionately from smaller cities. The Catholics comprised 25 per cent of the sample and were disproportionately from larger cities and lower-status families. Jews, who made up about 8 per cent of the sample, were almost all from larger cities, came from relatively high-status families, and showed superior academic performance.

Correlates of Career Choice

The dynamic processes involved in career choice are highly complex. Many of the elements involved are set in motion long before the youngster arrives at college and they continue and increase throughout the four years of college. The end result is that graduates in different major fields reveal significant differences in sex composition, academic performance, values, and socioeconomic background. Following are the characteristics which the National Opinion Research Center study found to be significantly associated with career choice.

Education. As shown in Table 2, approximately one third of the 1961 June graduates expected to teach primary and secondary grades. In addition to being the largest career group in the study, this field also demonstrated the largest gain through either change of major or declaration of a major by undecided students. Being a female was the prime factor associated with education and a service-value disposition—a desire to work with people rather than with things and a lack of desire to make a lot of money—was the second most frequently associated characteristic of the educators-to-be. Compared with the total graduating class, education majors were slightly lower in academic performance than the majors in medicine, the physical sciences, the social sciences, and the humanities. With respect to background characteristics, lower socioeconomic status and smaller hometowns both contributed to choice of education as a major.

Business. The second most popular field (see Table 2) was business, which showed a considerable increase from the freshman to the senior years. Business is a masculine major, in terms of original choice and change of majors. With respect to occupational val-

TABLE 2

DISTRIBUTION OF RESPONDENTS BY ANTICIPATED CAREER FIELD

	Per Cent	Per Cent
Arts and science fields		18.0
Physical science	5.4	
Biological science	2.1	
Social sciences	4.0	
Humanities	6.5	
Professional fields		59.3
Primary and secondary education	32.2	
Engineering	8.3	
Other health professions (other than medicine)	4.0	
Law	3.9	
Medicine	2.8	
Social work	1.8	
Other professions	6.3	
Other		19.7
Business and Administration	18.2	
Agricultural and related fields	1.5	
Respondent checked "Job which has no near equivalent in this list"		2.8
Total	99.8%	99.8%

Source: James A. Davis, *Great Expectations: Volume One* (Chicago: The University of Chicago: National Opinion Research Center, 1963), p. 145.

ues, a greater desire for high income and a lesser need for creativity in work were characteristic of the business majors. In most comparisons, seniors expecting to enter the business world were lower on academic performance than those with other career choices. Negroes were clearly less attracted to careers in business. Catholic students, when compared with Protestants and Jews, showed a greater inclination toward business. Interest in people, socioeconomic status, and size of hometown were not significantly associated with business as a career choice.

Social sciences. It is to be expected that all the remaining fields will contain a relatively small proportion of majors, because education and business together include over half (51.9 per cent) of the career choices. The social science majors were at least 10 per cent better in academic performance than students in education, business, biological sciences, other professions, and engineering. The characteristic pattern of occupational values revealed a broader range than that in other fields. There were many who had high interest in people, while others expressed low interest. Apparently, the fields of social science which do not involve face-to-face contact with people attract these low-interest-in-people majors. The data indicated that the money-oriented student avoided the social sciences. High socioeconomic backgrounds and larger hometowns are correlated with the choice of social science as a career; and Jews, on a proportionate basis, tend to overchoose this occupational goal.

Humanities and fine arts. Although the humanities contained only 6.5 per cent of the total number of students, this was still greater than the proportion in the social sciences and the physical sciences, and approximately the same as law and medicine combined. A desire for originality and the lack of a desire for money were outstanding qualities of the students in this major field; and they were high academic performers. Women chose this major more frequently than men. However, in terms of turnover of declared majors, women showed a net loss and men a net gain during the four years of college. Regardless of sex, academic performance, and value orientations, the seniors choosing the humanities tended to come from higher socioeconomic families.

Biological sciences. Generally, the research data produced very few relationships which differentiated the biological sciences majors from those in other fields. These students did show a lower interest in working with people.

Law. Even women with the appropriate academic performance, socioeconomic status, and value patterns seldom chose this field. Lawyers were characterized by a desire for a high income and little need for originality. These youngsters were also relatively high academic performers from relatively high-status families. Jews and Catholics tended to overchoose law in comparison with Protestants; and students from larger cities were similarly inclined. This can be explained in terms of the religious- and social-status composition of those students from the larger hometowns.

Physical sciences.   The physical sciences represented a major career cluster which showed the greatest loss of students during the four-year college period. For the most part, these majors had a low interest in people but a high concern with originality and creativity. Generally, men were more attracted to the physical sciences and, at graduation, these students demonstrated high academic performance averages. The losses to the physical sciences are concentrated, for the most part, among the coeds and people-oriented students; among men with the appropriate value patterns, and especially men of lower socioeconomic-status backgrounds, there are net increases.

Medicine.   The research showed a strong net movement out of medicine during the four-year college period. High academic performance was associated with movement toward a medical career. This factor showed a consistent relationship to freshman choice, retention of majors, and recruitment of new students. Women were less attracted to this field. Among men, the value of wanting to work with people without wanting to be original and creative was associated with the choice of medicine as a career orientation. With minor exceptions, this field drew from the higher socioeconomic-status groups. Religion was a factor among men, but not among women. Jewish males were highest on freshman choice and recruitment of new majors. When compared with Protestants, Catholics tended to be somewhat higher on freshman choice and retention, and no Protestant-Catholic differences were in evidence in recruitment. The size of hometown proved to be an erratic predictor: for men, it was not associated with freshman choice, but was positively related to higher percentages of Catholics and Jews remaining in this major; among women, freshman choice and retention were associated with being from larger hometowns.

Engineering.   This field showed the greatest net decline during the four years of college. This trend away from engineering could not be explained by differences in the values, sex, or social origins of the seniors, because the losses outnumbered the gains in each of these categories. The occupational values of low interest in people and high interest in opportunities for originality and creativity and making money provided the most distinguishing characteristics among these majors. The overwhelming percentage of majors are males (99 per cent at graduation) and they had a lower percentage of high academic performers than did the groups in social sciences, humanities, law, physical sciences, and medicine. Like the physical science majors, the engineering seniors showed a relatively low socioeconomic-status trend, while both Christians and Jews of high socioeconomic-status background revealed greater rates of defection. Negro and Jewish students were unlikely to major in engineering.

Career Choice: Change and Stability During College

Much shifting of career choice occurs during the college years. The data showed that 47 per cent of the seniors in the sample changed their majors during their college careers, 43 per cent made no change, and 10 per cent shifted from nonpreference to some specific field. In an evaluation of recruitment and loss, the occupations were grouped into three categories:[29]

1. *Gainers—Business and education:* the two fields with low losses, high gains, and net increases.
2. *Losers—medicine, engineering, physical sciences and other professions:* the fields with high loss rates, and recruitment rates insufficient to prevent a decline.
3. *Traders—social sciences, biological sciences, law, humanities:* the fields with high loss rates but recruitment rates which more than offset the defections.

Even with all this shifting, when the percentage distributions of choices for freshmen were compared with those for seniors, career preferences were surprisingly similar, with the greatest difference being in the proportionate increase in education majors (25 to 33 per cent). Generally the items which discriminated between the defectors and those who remained in the major were the same as those which differentiated the original recruits from the nonrecruits. The value orientations of students proved to be an extremely important factor involved in career change. For example, the freshman student majoring in business with little desire for a lot of money and much concern with opportunities to be original and creative is

---

[29] *Ibid.*, p. 167.

more likely to leave this field than the student who wants a lot of money and cares less about originality and creativity.

In perspective, the data did not suggest that the college experience was the overriding element in ultimate occupation choice. Rather, the conclusion was that these youth graduated with approximately the same job orientations they had as freshmen, and as other research indicates, the changes that did occur seemed to be a continuation of trends which began long before college entrance. But the data did show that the four years of college experience had some impact on career choice. As indicated above, almost half the graduates changed majors or chose a career while in college, and certain fields, such as engineering and medicine, do undergo a loss in popularity. Other changes are in evidence. For example, in the sphere of value orientations, when freshman majors were compared with graduating seniors, students majoring in other professions became slightly more people-oriented; those in the physical sciences moved away from pure originality to money and originality; those in the social sciences shifted from a basically people-oriented field toward a more originality-oriented field; those in law and medicine moved from an undifferentiated state to a money-and-people orientation. Other changes, such as the improvement in academic performance of the medical students over the four years and the defection of Negroes from business, also indicate that college experience may have some over-all effect on occupational career choice.

Allocation: The Business of College Placement

In its capacity as gatekeeper to the upper-middle-class occupations, the colleges and universities currently are called upon not only to do a fantastic job of screening, absorbing, and sorting some 3 million students, but they must also aid in the placement of their annual crop of some 400,000 graduates. The college placement office has become a very large and powerful force on the American college scene. Its impact is so recent that its function has received little attention by scholars. Everett W. Stephens, vividly illustrates this with the following episode:

> Just a dozen years ago the dean of one of New England's finest ivy-league colleges was asked what kind of job-placement services were available on his campus. His tart reply was that his particular

college considered it no more its business to help a graduate find a job than it did to help him find a wife![30]

Dean Stephens goes on to relate that this college now has an excellent counseling program with a full-time placement office which maintains placement contacts with hundreds of employers.

Industry, because of its dire need for high-level technicians and managers, has been the prime mover in this trend. This industrial need caused management to pressure college boards of trustees to earmark special funds for the establishment of placement offices. The college placement office generally has a twofold function: to assist graduates to find a job in the world of business, industry, and government, and to provide employers with the opportunity to contact and select potential employees. The present-day placement officer is indeed a harried man. He must provide sufficient office space in which hundreds of recruiting representatives from competing firms may interview thousands of student aspirants. The logistics of arranging the interview schedules alone, under the typical conditions of limited funds and space, challenges a tactician of the highest capabilities. Student records must be obtained and filed, faculty recommendations must be accumulated, and continuous liaison with company officials must be maintained.

All this is accomplished via piles of correspondence, innumerable telephone conversations, luncheons, and other devices. Recent articles appearing in the *Journal of College Placement* have expressed the desire for more efficiency in the whole operation. Dean Stephens wonders: ". . . why a company must visit 150 colleges a year and interview 3000 seniors to hire thirty? Or why an individual needs twenty-five interviews to find a suitable job?"[31]

Along these lines, Allan Rood,[32] is concerned with the fact that some 50 per cent of the college graduates recruited through campus interviews change jobs within one year. In order to make college placement more effective, the author suggests some type of non-credit course, possibly in the form of an elective seminar, which would prepare the student for effective placement. Other writers suggest that this type of orientation course be given to students throughout the four years of college.

---

[30] Everett W. Stephens, "Placement's Historic Need: Early Guidance," *Journal of College Placement,* XXII (February 1962), 73–74. Quote from p. 73.

[31] *Ibid.,* p. 74.

[32] Allan Rood, "The Paradox of Effective Recruiting," *Journal of College Placement,* XXII (February 1962), 35, 100, 102, 104.

There is little doubt that the placement and recruitment functions of the college placement office will become an increasingly important element in campus activity. As a result of this development, an increased professionalization of placement personnel will undoubtedly occur. This is already indicated by the titles currently given to placement officers. For example, many placement officials now are identified as "Director, Counseling and Placement Center," "Director of Placement and Guidance," or "Director of Student Personnel Services."

Some organizational structure will have to be developed to resolve the problem of whether the placement office exists primarily for the benefit of the student or for that of the corporation recruitment representative. It is obvious that, at times, from the point of view of the student, at least, a conflict of interest may arise. In the future, carefully delineated benchmarks must be established by both the faculty and administration in order to avoid potential inequities.

Index